Contents

UNIT 4

UNIT 5

To the Student

Vocabulary is a key that unlocks meaning and comprehension. It opens doors to new ideas. It helps you become a better reader, writer, and student.

In *Words to Learn By: Building Academic Vocabulary* you will learn 100 words. These words were carefully chosen for you. They are high-frequency academic words. What does high-frequency mean? It means you will find these words everywhere.

You will find them in textbooks and in reference books and on tests. You will also find these words in magazines, newspapers, and work-related materials. You will hear them in conversations at school or work, and on radio and television.

By learning these words, you will become a more successful student. These words will help you no matter what you are reading. They will also help you in classroom discussions and in your writing.

How to Use the Book

Words to Learn By: Building Academic Vocabulary has five units. Each unit includes four lessons. In each lesson you will learn five high-frequency words. First, the teacher will explain the meaning of each word and give examples. Then you will practice using the words.

It is important to use these words when you are not in class. Use them when you talk to friends and people at work. Listen for the words in conversations and on radio and television. If you are a parent, use the words with your children.

We believe that *Words to Learn By: Building Academic Vocabulary* will help you reach your academic goals. We wish you much success!

Stephen Dolainski and Elizabeth Griffin

Unit 1

brief
however
refer
item
perform
category
previous
effective
examine
ideal
essential
purpose
reflect
notice
select
similar
require
specific
task
topic

brief category effective essential perform specific

however similar purpose **item** examine ideal

perform **previous** refer notice brief essential

purpose essential require category **reflect** select

effective task **specific** however topic similar

Vocabulary Knowledge Rating Chart

How well do you know the words? Use the numbers to rate your knowledge of the vocabulary words. Follow the teacher's directions.

4 = I know the word. I know it well enough to teach it to someone else.
3 = The word is familiar. I think I know what it means.
2 = I have heard the word, but I'm not sure what it means.
1 = I don't know the word at all.

	My rating before instruction	I think the word means	My rating after instruction
brief			
item			
previous			
reflect			
specific			

Word Meaning Chart

Complete the chart. Follow the teacher's directions.

brief *(adjective)* /breef/
Something that is short in length or time is **brief**.

EXAMPLES

There was a _____ story in the newspaper about the city council meeting.

Class Example: _____

My Example: For me, a **brief** phone call takes _____ minutes.

item *(noun)* /AHY tem/
An **item** is one thing or object.

EXAMPLES

Ice cream is one _____ in the frozen food section of the grocery store.

Class Example: _____

My example: My favorite personal **item** of clothing is _____

previous *(adjective)* /PREE vee uhs/
The word **previous** tells that one thing happened before another.

EXAMPLES

Mr. Martin was the _____ owner of the large blue house.

Class Example: _____

My Example: The name of my **previous** teacher is _____

reflect *(verb)* /ri FLEKT/
To **reflect** on something means to think carefully about it.

EXAMPLES

The old woman sits in a chair and _____ on her long life.

Class Example: _____

My Example: An important experience I **reflect** on is _____

specific *(adjective)* /spi SIF ik/
The word **specific** means exact or clear.

EXAMPLES

You can get _____ driving directions on the Internet.

Class Example: _____

My Example: A **specific** brand of soft drink I like is _____

Use the Words

Complete each sentence. Write the correct form of the vocabulary word in the blank space.

1. Each student read a book and gave a _____ report to the class.

2. This store sells a _____ type of running shoe.

3. A flashlight is a useful _____ in an emergency.

4. Jonathan takes a walk when he needs to _____ on his day.

5. Esperanza's _____ apartment had a large swimming pool.

Complete the Sentences

These sentences have been started for you. They are not complete. Complete them with your own words.

1. Diana asked the manager at her previous job _____

_____

_____

2. Specific information I don't give to other people includes _____

_____

_____

_____

3. A good place for a brief visit in my city is _____

_____

_____

_____

4. When I reflect on my life, I _____

_____

_____

5. An item that I keep in my kitchen is _____

_____

_____

Words at Work

Circle the best answer to each multiple choice question below. Then write a brief response to the question that follows. Write your answers in complete sentences.

1. Dae-Ho has a job interview. He carefully chooses the items of clothing to wear to the interview. What does that tell you about Dae-Ho?

   (A) He does not have many clothes.　　**(B)** He likes his clothes.　　**(C)** He wants to look professional.

   What items of clothing would you choose for a job interview? _____

   _____

   _____

2. On a job application, the section marked "Previous Work Experience" is the place to include

   (A) the last school you attended.　　**(B)** the name of a coworker at your last job.　　**(C)** your position at your last job.

   What is another item of information you could include in the "Previous Work Experience"

   section? _____

   _____

   _____

3. Mr. Lopez was worried because his job interview was brief. How long was the interview?

   (A) 1 hour　　　　　　**(B)** 15 minutes　　　　　　**(C)** 2 hours

   Why was Mr. Lopez worried about the brief interview? _____

   _____

   _____

4. Marcos looks in the employee handbook to find specific information about

   (A) the birthdays of coworkers.　　**(B)** the amount of his next paycheck.　　**(C)** paid holidays.

   What other specific information can be found in an employee handbook? _____

   _____

   _____

   _____

Word Families

Most words are part of a family of words. Study the word families on this page. Then fill in the missing words in the sentences below using the words from this lesson. Use the correct form of each word to complete the sentences.

---

brief *(adjective)*

- briefly *(adverb)*
  They had lived in the city briefly, so they did not know it well.

item *(noun)*

- itemize *(verb)*
  The receipt itemized all the groceries Miranda bought.

previous *(adjective)*

- previously *(adverb)*
  He previously worked at the post office.

reflect *(verb)*

- reflection *(noun)*
  A holiday such as Thanksgiving is a time for reflection.

specific *(adjective)*

- specifically *(adverb)*
  The table was designed specifically for a flat-screen television.

---

1. Graduation offers many moments for _____.

2. Leticia didn't make much money last year because she only worked

   _____ at the restaurant.

3. Ms. Lee teaches chemistry now. She _____ taught biology.

4. The coach _____ told the players to arrive one hour before the game.

5. Isabel left a _____ message on the answering machine.

6. Jamal's _____ landlord helped him paint the apartment.

7. A doctor's appointment is made for a _____ day and time.

8. The test score report _____ every correct and incorrect answer.

9. Greg took a moment to _____ on the job he had done.

10. The apartment was _____ painted dark brown.

11. There are several new _____ in the lost and found box.

12. We had a _____ meeting before leaving for the day.

A fire, flood, or other emergency can happen any time. Are you prepared?

Exercise 5 What Do You Think?

Read each question and write a brief answer. Explain your answers in complete sentences.

1. Imagine you have less than one hour to leave your home because of an emergency. What items would you take with you? Would you take personal items like clothing or family items like photographs and important papers? Why would you take these items?

_____

_____

_____

2. Do you prefer working for a manager who gives brief and specific directions?

_____

_____

3. Is it helpful for a person to reflect on a previous time in his or her life? Why or why not?

_____

_____

Reading Connection

Read the following passage and answer the questions.

Who Is Barack Obama?

Most people know that Barack Obama is the first African-American president of the United States. How much do you know about this man? Where does he come from? What are some important events in his life?

His full name is Barack Hussein Obama. He was born in Hawaii on August 4, 1961. His mother was American. Her name was Ann Dunham. She grew up in a small town in Kansas. His father was from Kenya, a country in Africa. His name was also Barack. He grew up in a small village and took care of goats.

Barack's father went to college in Hawaii. He met Ann there, and they got married. A few years later, they were divorced. His father eventually moved back to Kenya. Barack and his mother stayed in Hawaii. Barack saw his father only one more time. His father died in 1982.

In 1966, Ann married a man from Indonesia. The new family moved to Jakarta, the capital of Indonesia. Barack lived there for five years. Then he moved back to Hawaii to live with his grandparents.

Barack enjoyed school in Hawaii and also learned to play basketball. There were only two other African-American students at his high school. During this time, he started to reflect on the importance of race in the United States.

After high school, Barack moved to New York City to go to college. Later, he went to Chicago to help low-income communities. He also went to Kenya to visit his father's grave and meet his relatives.

In 1988, Barack started Harvard Law School. The next summer he met Michelle Robinson while he was working in Chicago. They got married four years later.

He was elected to the Illinois State Senate in 1996. In 2004, he was elected to the United States Senate. He made history in 2008 when he was elected President of the United States.

1. Where did Barack Obama live after the brief marriage of his parents?

   _____

   _____

2. Barack Obama previously lived in Indonesia. How might his experience living in another country help him as president?

   _____

   _____

3. Why would a trip to Kenya cause Barack Obama to reflect on his family history?

   _____

   _____

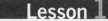

Lesson 1

brief category effective essential perform specific however similar purpose **item** examine ideal perform **previous** refer notice brief essential purpose essential require category **reflect** select effective task **specific** however topic similar

New Word List

☐ brief

☐ item

☐ previous

☐ reflect

☐ specific

Exercise 7 # Writing Connection

Write a brief response to each question. Use words from this lesson in your answer. Write your answers in complete sentences.

Think about one sport. Describe the specific skills needed to play that sport.

_____

_____

_____

_____

_____

Reflect on a time in your life that was important to you. Why was it important? Are you a different person today because of that time?

_____

_____

_____

_____

_____

_____

Exercise 8 # Reflection

Think about the words you have studied in this lesson.

---

1. Which words did you enjoy learning? _____

2. Select one word and imagine where you will use the word. Explain the situation.

_____

_____

3. Which words do you still need help with? _____

4. Return to the Knowledge Rating Chart at the beginning of this lesson. Complete column 3. How have your responses changed?

brief **category** effective essential perform
however similar item purpose examine ideal
perform previous **refer** notice brief essential
purpose essential require category reflect **select**
effective task however specific **topic** similar

Vocabulary Knowledge Rating Chart

How well do you know the words? Use the numbers to rate your knowledge of the vocabulary words. Follow the teacher's directions.

4 = I know the word. I know it well enough to teach it to someone else.
3 = The word is familiar. I think I know what it means.
2 = I have heard the word, but I'm not sure what it means.
1 = I don't know the word at all.

	My rating before instruction	I think the word means	My rating after instruction
category			
however			
refer			
select			
topic			

Word Meaning Chart

Complete the chart. Follow the teacher's directions.

---

category *(noun)* /KAT i gohr ee/

A **category** is a group of people or things that are the same kind.

EXAMPLES

Video games are a popular _____ of entertainment.

Class Example: _____

My Example: My favorite **category** of music is _____

---

however *(adverb)* /hou EV er/

The word **however** shows that what comes next is different from what was said or done before.

EXAMPLES

The weather report said it would be sunny. My father, _____, said it would rain.

Class Example: _____

My Example: My friends wanted to go to the movies. **However,** _____

---

refer *(verb)* /ri FUR/

To **refer** to something means to get information from it.

EXAMPLES

Mai had to _____ to the recipe when she was making the chicken dish.

Class Example: _____

My Example: When I need a phone number, I **refer** to _____

---

select *(verb)* /si LEKT/

To **select** means to choose.

EXAMPLES

It is important to _____ safe toys for children.

Class Example: _____

My Example: Something I think about when I **select** a gift is _____

---

topic *(noun)* /TOP ik/

A **topic** is a big idea or subject.

EXAMPLES

Love is the _____ of Valentine's Day cards.

Class Example: _____

My Example: A **topic** I like reading about is _____

Use the Words

Complete each sentence. Write the correct form of the vocabulary word in the blank space.

1. The judges will _____ the winner of the dance contest.

2. Kushal _____ to a map so that he won't get lost.

3. Talk shows are a popular _____ of television programs.

4. Crime was a _____ at the city council meeting.

5. Greta's car is old and uses a lot of gas. Stefan's car, _____, is newer and uses less gas.

Complete the Sentences

These sentences have been started for you. They are not complete. Complete them with your own words.

1. Some people don't think education is important. However, _____

    _____

    _____

2. In the category of team sports, I specifically like _____

    _____

    _____

3. When voters select someone for office, it is important _____

    _____

    _____

4. When grocery shopping, it is a good idea to refer to a shopping

    list because _____

    _____

    _____

5. A current topic discussed in government is _____

    _____

    _____

Words at Work

Circle the best answer to each multiple choice question below. Then write a brief response to the question that follows. Write your answers in complete sentences.

1. Ken and his friends discuss sports, politics, and other topics during their lunch break. What does this tell us about Ken and his friends?

   (A) They do not eat a big lunch.

   (B) They worry about everything.

   (C) They have many different interests.

   What is a topic you talk about at work or school? _____

   _____

   _____

2. Carlos has to deliver a package to a company in a building with ten floors. He does not know which floor the company is on. What can he refer to?

   (A) the building directory

   (B) a phone book

   (C) the newspaper

   What are some things you refer to when you are looking for a store or a restaurant?

   _____

   _____

   _____

3. Mitchell is reading the help wanted ads. He is looking for jobs in the sales and restaurants categories. However, he has never worked in a restaurant. What would you say to him?

   (A) Apply for all jobs.

   (B) Do not search for jobs in the help wanted ads.

   (C) Apply for jobs where you have the most experience.

   In what job category do you have the most experience? _____

   _____

   _____

4. Mrs. Hassan needs a new sign for her business. She gave Leo a list of companies that make signs and asked him to select one. What does this tell us about Mrs. Hassan?

   (A) She does not like Leo.

   (B) She trusts Leo.

   (C) She does not like her job.

   When have you asked someone to select something for you? _____

   _____

   _____

Word Families

Most words are part of a family of words. Study the word families on this page. Then fill in the missing words in the sentences below using the words from this lesson. Use the correct form of each word to complete the sentences.

---

category *(noun)*

- **categorize** *(verb)*
  Karina's job is to categorize the new books by topic.

refer *(verb)*

- **reference** *(noun)*
  A dictionary is a very helpful reference for students.

select *(verb)*

- **selection** *(noun)*
  The bakery has a nice selection of cakes and pastries.

1. The local library has a large _____ of books for children and young adults.

2. Sammy remembers the names of all the movies that have won the award in the

   _____ of Best Picture.

3. Do you know a good _____ for checking grammar and punctuation rules?

4. One way the U.S. Census _____ people is by age.

5. Gabrielle helped the customer _____ a new watch.

6. The cashier _____ to the price list for the correct cost of the item.

7. Can you help us _____ these sales records by year?

8. Remember to _____ to the test directions if needed.

9. There is a wide _____ of dogs to adopt.

10. Trucks are in a different _____ of vehicle than compact cars.

11. Maps and atlases are _____ we use in our history class.

12. Karen _____ the winner of the scholarship.

Selecting a name for a child is an important decision.

Exercise 5 What Do You Think?

Read each question and write a brief answer. Explain your answers in complete sentences.

1. Would you refer to a book of baby names to select a name for your child?

   _____

   _____

   _____

2. Do you think religion is a good topic to discuss at work?

   _____

   _____

   _____

3. When you buy music, do you make your selection based on the musician or the category of music?

   _____

   _____

   _____

The Calendar

Is there a calendar on the wall in your home, school, or workplace? Most people have one. The calendar marks the days, weeks, and months of the year. A year is one complete cycle of all the seasons, or one orbit of the earth around the sun.

Human beings have been using calendars for thousands of years. Calendars help people understand and record time. They help people know when the seasons are changing and how long each will last.

Today, everybody uses the same calendar. However, that was not always true in the past. Some people used a calendar that followed the cycles of the moon. Other people used a calendar based on the cycles of the sun. Early calendars did not always do the job well.

About 600 years ago, people decided it was a good idea to have a common calendar. The new calendar had a year with 365 days. The days were divided into 12 months. The new calendar did a better job of showing when the seasons came. It was not perfect, but it was better than the previous calendars.

To keep the new calendar on schedule with the seasons, an extra day was added every four years. Today, this fourth year is called a "leap year." Leap years are the only years when February 29 is on the calendar.

The new calendar was called the Gregorian calendar. It is named after Pope Gregory XIII. He ordered the changes to the calendar. Today, the Gregorian calendar is used by most people in the world.

1. In the past, why was it important for people to refer to a calendar?

_____

_____

_____

2. What are two categories of calendars people previously used?

_____

_____

_____

3. Why was it a good idea for people to select a common calendar to refer to?

_____

_____

_____

brief **category** effective essential perform
however similar item purpose examine ideal
perform previous **refer** notice brief essential
purpose essential require category reflect **select**
effective task however specific **topic** similar

New Word List

☐ category

☐ however

☐ refer

☐ select

☐ topic

Review Word List

☐ _____

☐ _____

☐ _____

☐ _____

☐ _____

Exercise 7 # Writing Connection

Write a brief response to each question. Use words from this lesson or the previous lesson in your answer. Write your answers in complete sentences.

Reflect on when you were a child. What specific topic interested you? Why did that topic interest you?

_____

_____

_____

_____

_____

Select two people you know well. Write about two ways these people are different from each other. (Use the vocabulary word *however* in your answer.)

_____

_____

_____

_____

_____

Exercise 8 # Reflection

Think about the words you have studied in this lesson.

1. Which words did you enjoy learning? _____

2. Select one word and imagine where you will use the word. Explain the situation.

_____

_____

3. Which words do you still need help with? _____

4. Return to the Knowledge Rating Chart at the beginning of this lesson. Complete column 3. How have your responses changed?

brief category **effective** essential perform
however similar item purpose **examine** ideal
perform previous refer **notice** brief essential
purpose ideal essential require reflect select
effective task however specific topic **similar**

Vocabulary Knowledge Rating Chart

How well do you know the words? Use the numbers to rate your knowledge of the vocabulary words. Follow the teacher's directions.

4 = I know the word. I know it well enough to teach it to someone else.
3 = The word is familiar. I think I know what it means.
2 = I have heard the word, but I'm not sure what it means.
1 = I don't know the word at all.

	My rating before instruction	I think the word means	My rating after instruction
effective			
examine			
notice			
purpose			
similar			

Word Meaning Chart

Complete the chart. Follow the teacher's directions.

effective *(adjective)* /ih FEK tiv/ — To be **effective** is to get a positive result.

EXAMPLES

Aspirin is an _____ pain killer.

Class Example: _____

My Example: An **effective** way for me to remember things is _____

examine *(verb)* /ig ZAM in/ — To **examine** means to look at something carefully.

EXAMPLES

A doctor _____ people who are hurt or sick.

Class Example: _____

My Example: Police **examine** a crime scene for _____

notice *(verb)* /noh TIS/ — To **notice** is to see, feel, smell, or hear something or someone.

EXAMPLES

Parents usually _____ when their children come home late.

Class Example: _____

My Example: I **notice** that when I'm tired, I _____

purpose *(noun)* /PUR puhs/ — A **purpose** is the reason for something.

EXAMPLES

The _____ of studying vocabulary is to learn more words.

Class Example: _____

My Example: My **purpose** for saving money now is _____

similar *(adjective)* /SIM uh ler/ — The word **similar** means almost the same, but not exactly.

EXAMPLES

Lemons and limes are _____ kinds of fruit.

Class Example: _____

My Example: The United States and Canada are **similar** because _____

Use the Words

Complete each sentence. Write the correct form of the vocabulary word in the blank space.

1. One _____ of exercise is to become stronger.

2. The students thought Mr. Nelson was an _____ teacher because he explained things clearly.

3. Did you _____ the strong smell of perfume on the elevator?

4. Mrs. Schultz carefully _____ each piece of fruit before she bought it.

5. Two cars that are _____ in size may have very different prices.

Complete the Sentences

These sentences have been started for you. They are not complete. Complete them with your own words.

1. My purpose for reading the newspaper is _____

2. Natalie wants a work schedule similar to her husband's so that _____

3. I examined the wall in the kitchen to _____

4. Martha was happy when her friend noticed _____

5. An effective way to lose weight is _____

Words at Work

Circle the best answer to each multiple choice question below. Then write a brief response to the question that follows. Write your answers in complete sentences.

---

1. Professor Khan always explains the purpose of an activity to her students. Why does she do that?

   (A) She thinks her students are bored.

   (B) She thinks her students can't follow directions.

   (C) She wants her students to understand.

   When have you had to explain the purpose of a job or activity to someone else? _____

   _____

   _____

2. Lydia's supervisor notices that she usually comes to work early. She also notices that Lydia never complains when she is asked to work overtime. The supervisor is happy with Lydia's work. What is something her supervisor could do?

   (A) give her a raise

   (B) give her more work to do

   (C) change her schedule

   What is something you would want your supervisor or teacher to notice about you?

   _____

   _____

3. The new employee watched Mr. Garcia with customers. He thought Mr. Garcia was an effective salesperson because

   (A) the customers smiled.

   (B) the customers bought more items.

   (C) the customers thanked him.

   What are some things an effective salesperson does? _____

   _____

   _____

4. A supervisor examined the high number of accidents in a factory. What was her purpose?

   (A) to find the cause of the accidents

   (B) to find the cost of new machines

   (C) to find the reasons for parking problems

   What problem would you like to see examined at your work or school? _____

   _____

   _____

Exercise 4 | Word Families

Most words are part of a family of words. Study the word families on this page. Then fill in the missing words in the sentences below using the words from this lesson. Use the correct form of each word to complete the sentences.

effective (adjective)

- effect (noun)
  High gasoline prices can have a negative effect on the auto industry.

- effectiveness (noun)
  The effectiveness of some cancer drugs is not certain.

- effectively (adverb)
  The musician effectively communicated his ideas through music.

examine (verb)

- examination (noun)
  The dentist's examination of Arlette's teeth was brief but complete.

- exam (noun)
  Louis passed his U.S. History exam because he studied for a week.

notice (verb)

- notice (noun)
  The owner of the laundromat posted a notice about the new hours.

- noticeable (adjective)
  The smell of fried fish was noticeable everywhere in the house.

purpose (noun)

- on purpose (idiom)
  The fire in the empty building was started on purpose.

similar (adjective)

- similarity (noun)
  There are many similarities between the Spanish and Italian languages.

1. Have you ever heard of a baseball team losing a game _____?

2. The mayor won the election because of his _____ as a leader.

3. Edgar was pleased with the _____ improvement on his test scores.

4. News of the election had a positive _____ on the country.

5. The Franklins got a _____ in the mail about a change in their credit card interest rate.

6. An _____ of the car showed that it had been scratched.

7. The _____ between the twin brothers often caused confusion.

Notices are put up to give people important information about road conditions.

Exercise 5 What Do You Think?

Read each question and write a brief answer. Explain your answers in complete sentences.

1. Is a notice on the street like the one in the picture the most effective way to give people important information?

    _____

    _____

    _____

2. Do you think it would be effective to examine each student's backpack every day for security reasons?

    _____

    _____

    _____

3. Do men and women have similar purposes when they buy flowers?

    _____

    _____

    _____

Reading Connection

Read the following passage and answer the questions.

Dr. Elizabeth Blackwell—America's First Female Doctor

At one time, there were no female medical doctors in the United States. Only men were doctors. However, Elizabeth Blackwell changed that. She was born in England in 1821. She would become the first woman to graduate from medical school and become a doctor.

Elizabeth's parents moved to America when she was 11. Her father died several years later. Elizabeth, her mother, and her sisters needed to support themselves. They opened a private school in Cincinnati.

At first, Elizabeth was not interested in medicine. She became a teacher. She soon learned that a close friend was dying. She told Elizabeth she wished her doctor were a woman. That is when Elizabeth became interested in medicine. She decided to go to medical school.

Elizabeth found that medical schools did not accept women as students. However, Geneva Medical College in New York allowed the students to decide whether Elizabeth could attend school there. The students were all men and thought it was a joke. They voted to let Elizabeth enter the college. In 1847, Elizabeth became the first woman in the United States to attend medical school.

Elizabeth graduated in 1849 with her medical degree. Hospitals, however, would not hire her. Landlords would not rent an office to her. So, she began to see women and children in her home. In 1857, she started a special hospital in New York City for women and children. Elizabeth also dreamed of opening a medical school for women. She started the Women's Medical College in 1868.

Today, there are female doctors in all areas of medicine. Elizabeth Blackwell was the pioneer who helped to make that possible.

1. Elizabeth had a friend who was dying. What effect did this have on Elizabeth?

_____

_____

_____

2. What was Elizabeth's purpose when she started a hospital for women and children?

_____

_____

_____

3. Elizabeth worked hard to become a doctor. In what other job categories have women had similar experiences?

_____

_____

brief category **effective** essential perform
however similar item purpose **examine** ideal
perform previous refer **notice** brief essential
purpose ideal essential require reflect select
effective task however specific topic **similar**

New Word List

☐ effective

☐ examine

☐ notice

☐ purpose

☐ similar

Review Word List

☐ _____

☐ _____

☐ _____

☐ _____

☐ _____

Writing Connection

Write a brief response to each question. Use words from this lesson or previous lessons in your answer. Write your answers in complete sentences.

Reflect on the problem of homelessness in your community. Describe two or three specific ways to effectively change the situation.

_____

_____

_____

_____

_____

Is it important for a person to have a purpose in life? Explain.

_____

_____

_____

_____

_____

Reflection

Think about the words you have studied in this lesson.

1. Which words did you enjoy learning? _____

2. Select one word and imagine where you will use the word. Explain the situation.

_____

_____

3. Which words do you still need help with? _____

4. Return to the Knowledge Rating Chart at the beginning of this lesson. Complete column 3. How have your responses changed?

brief category effective **essential** perform
however similar item purpose examine **ideal**
perform previous refer notice brief essential
purpose essential **require** item reflect select
effective **task** however specific topic similar

Vocabulary Knowledge Rating Chart

How well do you know the words? Use the numbers to rate your knowledge of the vocabulary words. Follow the teacher's directions.

4 = I know the word. I know it well enough to teach it to someone else.
3 = The word is familiar. I think I know what it means.
2 = I have heard the word, but I'm not sure what it means.
1 = I don't know the word at all.

	My rating before instruction	I think the word means	My rating after instruction
essential			
ideal			
perform			
require			
task			

Word Meaning Chart

Complete the chart. Follow the teacher's directions.

essential (adjective) /uh SEN shuhl/

Something that is **essential** is important and necessary.

EXAMPLES

Exercise is _____ for good health.

Class Example: _____

My Example: It is **essential** for me to get _____ hours of sleep.

ideal (adjective) /ahy DEE uhl/

The word **ideal** means perfect or almost perfect.

EXAMPLES

Sunshine is _____ weather for a day at the beach.

Class Example: _____

My Example: An **ideal** school has _____

perform (verb) /per FAWRM/

To **perform** means to do an action or job.

EXAMPLES

The soldier _____ his military service with courage.

Class Example: _____

My Example: I **perform** well on a test when _____

require (verb) /ri KWAHY uhr/

To **require** means to make something necessary.

EXAMPLES

The law in some states _____ everyone in a car to wear a seat belt.

Class Example: _____

My Example: I am **required** to show my student ID when _____

task (noun) /tahsk/

A **task** is a specific activity or job that needs to be done.

EXAMPLES

Preparing lessons is a _____ many teachers do at home.

Class Example: _____

My Example: A **task** I usually do on weekends is _____

Use the Words

Complete each sentence. Write the correct form of the vocabulary word in the blank space.

1. Dr. Rosen _____ the operation on my father's heart.

2. A comfortable pair of shoes is _____ to run a marathon.

3. Mrs. Ling broke her arm. A simple _____ like getting dressed was difficult.

4. An _____ neighborhood is safe and quiet.

5. The hospital _____ all visitors to sign in and get a badge.

Exercise 2 # Complete the Sentences

These sentences have been started for you. They are not complete. Complete them with your own words.

1. A job that requires a driver's license is _____

   _____

   _____

2. Before I leave my home, it is essential _____

   _____

   _____

3. It's difficult to perform a job well if _____

   _____

   _____

4. A task I often need help with is _____

   _____

   _____

5. On an ideal Sunday afternoon, _____

   _____

   _____

   _____

Words at Work

Circle the best answer to each multiple choice question below. Then write a brief response to the question that follows. Write your answers in complete sentences.

1. Carmen tells her friends that her job is in an ideal location. What is probably true for Carmen?

   (A) She takes two buses to work.

   (B) She lives two blocks from work.

   (C) She starts work at 9:30.

   What would be an ideal job location for you? _____

   _____

   _____

2. Tony works in a cafeteria kitchen. The law requires all kitchen workers to wear a hairnet. Tony has forgotten his hairnet three times this week. What does that tell us about Tony?

   (A) He is not responsible.

   (B) He does not work hard.

   (C) He is not friendly.

   Why is it important to know what is required of you at work? _____

   _____

   _____

3. Filing is a task that Bertha does not like. Which piece of information about Bertha is probably true?

   (A) Bertha files quickly.

   (B) Bertha thinks filing is boring.

   (C) Bertha offers to do filing for her coworkers.

   What is a task at school or work that you don't like? Why not? _____

   _____

   _____

4. Jack is a new employee. He wants to know if he is performing his job well. What should he do?

   (A) ask his customers

   (B) read his employee handbook

   (C) ask his manager

   How do you know if you are performing your job or schoolwork well? _____

   _____

   _____

   _____

Word Families

Most words are part of a family of words. Study the word families on this page. Then fill in the missing words in the sentences below using the words from this lesson. Use the correct form of each word to complete the sentences.

---

essential *(adjective)*
• essentials *(noun)* *Keep water and other essentials nearby in case of an emergency.*

perform *(verb)*
• performance *(noun)* *He got a raise because his job performance was excellent.*

require *(verb)*
• requirement *(noun)* *A high school diploma is a requirement for many jobs.* • required *(adjective)* *Ms. Luna forgot to bring the required documents to the meeting.*

1. The owners of the team were unhappy with the coach's _____,
   so they replaced him.

2. Wheat is an _____ ingredient in most breads.

3. Mr. Han's papers did not have the _____ signatures, so he did not
   get the loan.

4. The scientist _____ the experiment while his assistant watched.

5. What time do Joe's parents _____ him to be home?

6. One of the _____ to be president is to be born in the
   United States.

7. The store manager told the employees that it is _____ to treat
   customers with respect.

8. The car's _____ is better on the highway than in the city.

9. Hikers save space in their backpacks by carrying only the _____.

10. Did a minister or a judge _____ your sister's wedding?

11. A vice-principal _____ many duties in the school district.

12. Lee met all of the _____ to be a paramedic.

Many schools now require students to wear uniforms.

Exercise 5 What Do You Think?

Read each question and write a brief answer. Explain your answers in complete sentences.

1. Do you think students who are required to wear uniforms perform better in school?

_____

_____

_____

2. In an ideal marriage, should each partner be willing to perform every household task?

_____

_____

_____

3. Do you believe that the essential requirement of life is to take care of yourself and your family?

_____

_____

_____

Reading Connection

Read the following passage and answer the questions.

An Essential Tool for Life Today

How are a gas station, a library, and a bank similar to each other? They all use a computer. A computer at the gas station measures the amount of gas you put into your car. The computer at the library makes a record of the book you borrow and when you need to return it. Bank computers keep track of your money.

The first computers were used by the U.S. government during World War II. These computers were very large. One computer filled an entire room. It required several people to operate it.

Computers today, however, can sit on your desk or fit in your backpack. The computer is now an essential item in everyday life. Computers help make our lives easier and safer. Computers make traffic lights change from red to green. Doctors and hospitals use computers to help people who are ill. We even get cash from a computer at the ATM.

Computers can do things faster than people can. Cashiers at the grocery store used to put the price of each item into the cash register. Now a computer scans the price from a bar code on the item. In an instant, the computer adds up the prices, and we see the total on the screen.

Many jobs today require people to use computers. At home, millions of people use a computer every day. They use it to pay bills, communicate with friends and family, do homework, and even play games.

The computer is an essential tool and is here to stay.

1. Were the first computers similar to computers of today? Explain your answer.

_____

_____

_____

2. Why are computer skills required for so many jobs today?

_____

_____

_____

3. What specific tasks does a computer help you to perform?

_____

_____

_____

brief category effective **essential** perform
however similar item purpose examine **ideal**
perform previous refer notice brief essential
purpose essential **require** item reflect select
effective **task** however specific topic similar

New Word List

☐ essential

☐ ideal

☐ perform

☐ require

☐ task

Review Word List

☐ _____

☐ _____

☐ _____

☐ _____

☐ _____

Writing Connection

Write a brief response to each question. Use words from this lesson or previous lessons in your answer. Write your answers in complete sentences.

Describe your ideal vacation. Where would you go? What would you be doing? Would you travel alone or with someone?

_____

_____

_____

_____

_____

Shayla and Marcus are new parents. They both work, so they must find a babysitter for their child. What are the essential requirements for a child care provider? Give Shayla and Marcus your advice to help them with their task.

_____

_____

_____

_____

Reflection

Think about the words you have studied in this lesson.

1. Which words did you enjoy learning? _____

2. Select one word and imagine where you will use the word. Explain the situation.

_____

_____

3. Which words do you still need help with? _____

4. Return to the Knowledge Rating Chart at the beginning of this lesson. Complete column 3. How have your responses changed?

Activity 1 Ask Questions

Look at the picture of President Barack Obama. Imagine you are going to interview him. Write at least five questions you want to ask him. Use one or more of the vocabulary words you have studied in each question. <u>Underline</u> each vocabulary word you use. Some of your questions can begin with *Who, What, When, Where, Why,* or *How.*

Example: What is the most <u>essential</u> <u>task</u> the president must do?

WORD BANK

BRIEF
CATEGORY
EFFECTIVE
ESSENTIAL
EXAMINE
HOWEVER
IDEAL
ITEM
NOTICE
PERFORM
PREVIOUS
PURPOSE
REFER
REFLECT
REQUIRE
SELECT
SIMILAR
SPECIFIC
TASK
TOPIC

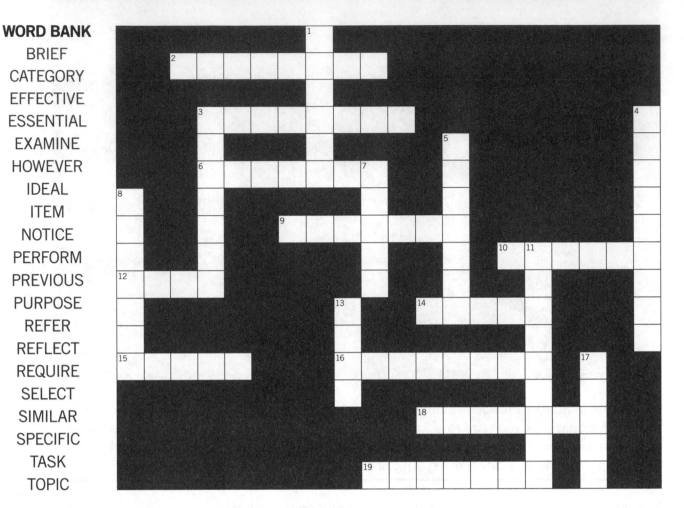

Activity 2 Puzzle

ACROSS

2. The _____ of Best Actress is my favorite.
3. Our _____ neighbor had a big dog.
6. I like to _____ on the words I have learned.
9. What's the _____ of this project?
10. Please _____ the color and style you want.
12. A bowl is a kitchen _____.
14. The _____ meeting lasted only 20 minutes.
15. If you forget, you can _____ to your notes.
16. I need the _____ time and place for the next meeting.
18. Does your job _____ you to wear a uniform?
19. The doctor needs to _____ your back.

DOWN

1. Did you _____ if the light was on?
3. I always _____ my job well.
4. Water is _____ to live.
5. I got up late. _____, I arrived on time.
7. The _____ of conversation was education.
8. The two brothers have _____ interests.
11. Do you know an _____ way to stop smoking?
13. Making my bed is a _____ I do every morning.
17. There is no war in an _____ world.

Activity 3 Synonyms

Complete these sentences. Use the correct form of the vocabulary word that means the same as the word in parentheses.

Example: Did you _____notice_____ (*see*) the new sign in the front of the building?

1. Jaime is short. _____, (*but*) he runs faster than anyone on the team.

2. Our team has not _____ (*chosen*) a captain yet.

3. Doing laundry is a boring but necessary _____ (*job*).

Activity 4 Antonyms

Complete these sentences. Use the correct form of the vocabulary word that means the opposite of the word or words in parentheses.

Example: It is _____essential_____ (*unimportant*) to water your plants regularly.

1. Dianne is _____ (*different from*) to her sister. They are both tall and thin.

2. In an _____ (*not perfect*) world, no one would be hungry.

3. The meeting was _____, (*long*) so I got home before the traffic started.

Activity 5 Practice Grammar with New Vocabulary

Rewrite the sentences. Change the <u>underlined</u> word or words from plural to singular.
Change other words from plural to singular as necessary.

Example: <u>They</u> always refer to their dictionaries when they are not sure how to spell a word.
Lorna always *refers* to *her* dictionary when *she is* not sure how to spell a word.

1. <u>Jill and Josh's</u> new apartment is similar to their previous apartment. _____

_____

2. The <u>men</u> are required to wear their jackets during the ceremony. _____

_____

3. What specific items do <u>they</u> need for their party next week? _____

_____

4. The <u>examinations</u> were brief. However, they were effective. _____

_____

Unit 2

through
consider
reject
increase
available
approval
challenge
benefit
physical
expect
option
focus
quite
decrease
possess
major
adequate
demonstrate
evaluate
release

benefit demonstrate adequate available quite
increase benefit approval **challenge** focus
option **expect** major consider demonstrate
decrease possess focus **physical** reject
quite adequate **release** through evaluate

Vocabulary Knowledge Rating Chart

How well do you know the words? Use the numbers to rate your knowledge of the vocabulary words. Follow the teacher's directions.

4 = I know the word. I know it well enough to teach it to someone else.
3 = The word is familiar. I think I know what it means.
2 = I have heard the word, but I'm not sure what it means.
1 = I don't know the word at all.

	My rating before instruction	I think the word means	My rating after instruction
benefit			
challenge			
expect			
physical			
release			

Word Meaning Chart

Complete the chart. Follow the teacher's directions.

benefit *(noun)* /BEN uh fit/ — A **benefit** is something that improves life.

EXAMPLES

A healthy heart is a _____ of regular exercise.

Class Example: _____

My Example: A **benefit** of having a high school diploma is _____

challenge *(noun)* /CHAL inj/ — A **challenge** is something that is difficult.

EXAMPLES

Learning to use a computer is a _____ for many people.

Class Example: _____

My Example: At school, _____ is a **challenge** for me.

expect *(verb)* /ik SPEKT/ — To **expect** means to have a good reason to believe something will happen.

EXAMPLES

Anna has all the credits she needs, so she _____ to graduate in June.

Class Example: _____

My Example: I **expect** my classmates to_____

physical *(adjective)* /FIZ i kuhl/ — The word **physical** relates to the movement or feeling of the body; or to something that can be seen or touched.

EXAMPLES

The paramedics performed a quick _____ examination of the boy.

Class Example: _____

My Example: A **physical** activity I enjoy is _____

release *(verb)* /ree LEES/ — To **release** means to free or let go of something or someone.

EXAMPLES

Dr. Williams may _____ Richard from the hospital tomorrow.

Class Example: _____

My Example: I **release** my stress by _____

Exercise 1 Use the Words

Complete each sentence. Write the correct form of the vocabulary word in the blank space.

1. It was a _____ to keep Kendra's birthday party a surprise.

2. The Recreation Department _____ the park to be open by summer.

3. The _____ changes in Henry from his weight loss surprised everyone.

4. Mrs. Weston gave the doctor permission to _____ her medical records.

5. A _____ of Sarah's new job is that the company pays for her health insurance.

Exercise 2 Complete the Sentences

These sentences have been started for you. They are not complete. Complete them with your own words.

1. When I was a child, my parents expected me to _____

   _____

   _____

2. One benefit of eating healthy foods is _____

   _____

   _____

3. The children were released early from school because _____

   _____

   _____

4. It's a challenge for me to study when _____

   _____

   _____

5. When I have physical pain, I _____

   _____

   _____

Words at Work

Circle the best answer to each multiple choice question below. Then write a brief response to the question that follows. Write your answers in complete sentences.

1. Leaving the house to get to work on time is a challenge for Alicia. What may be the reason?

   (A) She does not have an alarm clock.   **(B)** She has three young children.   **(C)** She eats a big breakfast.

   Is it a challenge for you to get to work or school on time? Why? _____

   _____

   _____

2. Adam is happy to work at night. He thinks it offers him several benefits. One of the benefits is that

   (A) he can take his daughter to school in the morning.   **(B)** he can eat dinner at work.   **(C)** he gets home late.

   What is the ideal work shift or school schedule for you? What benefits does it offer you?

   _____

   _____

   _____

3. Christina wants to know if the employees in her department are expected to give their manager a holiday gift. Which answer is probably true?

   (A) Yes, but only if the employee is new.   **(B)** Yes. It is important to show respect.   **(C)** No. It is not required.

   Should a manager expect a gift from workers? Explain your answer. _____

   _____

   _____

4. The company was required by law to meet the needs of workers with physical disabilities. What did the company do?

   (A) It put in an elevator.   **(B)** It covered the windows.   **(C)** It bought a new coffee machine.

   Name two other things schools and businesses can do to help people with physical disabilities.

   _____

   _____

Word Families

Most words are part of a family of words. Study the word families on this page. Then fill in the missing words in the sentences below using the words from this lesson. Use the correct form of each word to complete the sentences.

---

benefit *(noun)*

- benefit *(verb)*
  The new tax laws benefit both workers and business owners.

challenge *(noun)*

- challenging *(adjective)*
  Chess is a challenging game.

expect *(verb)*

- expectation *(noun)*
  The fans have high expectations for their basketball team.
- expected *(adjective)*
  The expected snowstorm closed the airport.

physical *(adjective)*

- physically *(adverb)*
  The scientist physically examined the rocks.

release *(verb)*

- release *(noun)*
  Everyone was waiting for the release of the test scores.

---

1. Frank's _____ of winning the lottery is not realistic.

2. It is _____ to create a schedule that makes everyone happy.

3. When is the _____ of the new space movie?

4. We were prepared for the _____ delay at the train station.

5. Nina _____ the bird from its cage every evening.

6. We were _____ and mentally tired after the long trip.

7. Everyone _____ from the new street lights because the neighborhood was safer.

8. A hug is a form of _____ contact.

9. What is the _____ of owning a car in a city with public transportation?

10. It was a _____ to paint the whole house in one week.

11. Louis did not _____ the weather to change so quickly.

Tennis requires physical skill and mental focus.

What Do You Think?

Read each question and write a brief answer. Explain your answers in complete sentences.

1. Is physical activity more effective than mental activity to release stress and tension? Explain your answer.

_____

_____

_____

2. Do children benefit when parents and teachers have high expectations of them?

_____

_____

_____

3. Do people benefit from having many challenges in life?

_____

_____

_____

Read the following passage and answer the questions.

Diary of a Pioneer Woman

In 1852, four families left Missouri for California. The trip took seven months. They traveled in covered wagons called prairie schooners. Sarah's diary tells part of the story.

Monday, April 5

We leave today for California. We are 39 souls heading into the unknown. I don't want to go. Don tells us our life will be better in the West. I pray we will all live to see a safe end to our long and dangerous journey.

Thursday, May 13

A terrible accident happened today. Little Zachariah Campbell fell out of his family's wagon and was lost. He was six. His mother Veranda is heart-broken. She cried all night.

Saturday, June 19

The trip is harder than I imagined. We travel for hours each day but sometimes go only a few miles. My hands are full of blisters. Our clothes are dirty, and our boots are muddy. There are insects everywhere. We are all so tired. I am worried we will not have enough food for the entire trip.

Friday, July 9

My little one, Eliza, is sick. She coughs and coughs. The tent is not warm, even in summer. The night sky is brilliant with stars.

Monday, August 23

We had to cross a deep mountain stream today. Our wagon was too heavy. The beautiful rocking chair my father made for us as a wedding gift now sits alone and empty in the wilderness.

Sunday, September 12

Today was a joyful day. Mrs. Rucker's baby was born at dawn. A healthy, beautiful child! Tonight we celebrate. We will sing and laugh.

Thursday, October 7

We have arrived! My family has survived the journey. We can begin our new life together in this place called California.

1. What are some of the physical and mental challenges Sarah describes in her diary?

_____

_____

2. Reflect on Sarah's experience. Can you see yourself on this journey? Would you be prepared for similar challenges?

_____

_____

_____

benefit demonstrate adequate available quite increase benefit approval **challenge** focus option **expect** major consider demonstrate decrease possess focus **physical** reject quite adequate **release** through evaluate

New Word List

☐ benefit

☐ challenge

☐ expect

☐ physical

☐ release

Review Word List

☐ _____

☐ _____

☐ _____

☐ _____

☐ _____

Writing Connection

Write a brief response to each question. Use words from this lesson or previous lessons in your answer. Write your answers in complete sentences.

Describe a previous challenge you had. Was it physical or mental? What did you do? How did you feel?

_____

_____

_____

_____

_____

Stanley, a friend and coworker, told you that he is thinking about quitting his job and working for himself. What can Stanley expect if he works for himself? How would Stanley benefit from working for himself?

_____

_____

_____

_____

_____

Reflection

Think about the words you have studied in this lesson.

1. Which words did you enjoy learning? _____

2. Select one word and imagine where you will use the word. Explain the situation.

_____

_____

3. Which words do you still need help with? _____

4. Return to the Knowledge Rating Chart at the beginning of this lesson. Complete column 3. How have your responses changed?

benefit **demonstrate** adequate available
increase challenge benefit approval focus
option expect **major** consider demonstrate
decrease possess focus physical **reject**
quite adequate release **through** evaluate

Vocabulary Knowledge Rating Chart

How well do you know the words? Use the numbers to rate your knowledge of the vocabulary words. Follow the teacher's directions.

4 = I know the word. I know it well enough to teach it to someone else.
3 = The word is familiar. I think I know what it means.
2 = I have heard the word, but I'm not sure what it means.
1 = I don't know the word at all.

	My rating before instruction	I think the word means	My rating after instruction
demonstrate			
increase			
major			
reject			
through			

Word Meaning Chart

Complete the chart. Follow the teacher's directions.

demonstrate (verb) /DEM uhn strayt/ To demonstrate is to show something clearly.

EXAMPLES

The students' high test scores _____ improvement.

Class Example: _____

My Example: I can **demonstrate** how to _____

increase (verb) /in KREES/ To increase is to grow larger in number, size, or quantity.

EXAMPLES

The price of gas _____ from $3.00 to $3.15 per gallon this month.

Class Example: _____

My Example: It is never popular to **increase** _____

major (adjective) /MEY jer/ The word major means very large, serious, or important.

EXAMPLES

The Appalachians are one of the _____ mountain ranges in the U.S.

Class Example: _____

My Example: A **major** topic of conversation with my friends is _____

reject (verb) /ri JEKT/ To reject means to refuse to accept something.

EXAMPLES

The judge _____ the request for a new trial.

Class Example: _____

My Example: A teacher **rejects** homework because _____

through (preposition) /throo/ The word through means going from one end to another end.

EXAMPLES

You have to go _____ the kitchen to get to the bathroom.

Class Example: _____

My Example: When I can't find my sweater, I look **through** _____

Use the Words

Complete each sentence. Write the correct form of the vocabulary word in the blank space.

1. The student council voted to _____ the price of dance tickets.

2. Bob's neighbor _____ his offer to build a new fence between their houses.

3. Make sure you read _____ all the papers before you sign them.

4. Smoking is a _____ cause of many cancers.

5. The number of accidents _____ a need for a stop sign at the intersection.

Exercise 2 # Complete the Sentences

These sentences have been started for you. They are not complete. Complete them with your own words.

1. A major benefit of living in my city is _____

2. When I walk through a shopping mall, I _____

3. I reject the idea that _____

4. If I were the principal of a school, I would increase _____

5. I demonstrate that I am responsible by _____

Circle the best answer to each multiple choice question below. Then write a brief response to the question that follows. Write your answers in complete sentences.

---

1. The workers were told that they could park in the lot next to the restaurant on Fridays through Mondays. Which of the following is true?

   (A) They cannot park there on Monday.

   (B) They can park there on Sunday.

   (C) They can park there on Thursday.

   Do you like to work Monday through Friday? How would you change your schedule? _____

   _____

   _____

2. Sally and Sharon do the same job. Their manager increased Sally's hours but not Sharon's. What was a major reason for the manager's decision?

   (A) Sally works more quickly than Sharon.

   (B) Sally makes coffee for everyone.

   (C) Sally is popular with her coworkers.

   Imagine the length of your work or school day increased. How would that change your life?

   _____

   _____

3. Kim and Carol sent the owners of their company a proposal for a child care center. The proposal was rejected. What might be the reason?

   (A) There were not enough toys.

   (B) The building insurance does not cover children.

   (C) The building has too many windows.

   What do you do when your suggestions at work or school are rejected? How do you feel?

   _____

   _____

4. An examination of company records demonstrated that some of their files were not complete. The examiners found that the documents

   (A) were missing.

   (B) were old.

   (C) were organized.

   What demonstrates to you that a person is organized? _____

   _____

   _____

Exercise 4 — Word Families

Most words are part of a family of words. Study the word families on this page. Then fill in the missing words in the sentences below using the words from this lesson. Use the correct form of each word to complete the sentences.

demonstrate *(verb)*
- demonstration *(noun)*
  The demonstration of the new phone system took an hour.

increase *(verb)*
- increase *(noun)*
  We noticed an increase in prices on the new menu.

reject *(verb)*
- rejection *(noun)*
  Dr. Harris was surprised when she received a rejection letter from the university.

through *(preposition)*
- through *(adjective)*
  Jefferson Boulevard is closed to through traffic this week because of road construction.

1. The police officer _____ my explanation and gave me a ticket.

2. During the busy winter holidays, many businesses _____ the number of workers.

3. Do you know if Overland Drive is a _____ street?

4. The long lines _____ the need for more cashiers at the grocery store.

5. Some people _____ the idea that the government should protect the environment.

6. We expect a _____ of how to use the camera before we buy it.

7. The _____ of the housing plan was a big disappointment for our community.

8. We had extra time, so we took the road that went _____ the park.

9. There was an _____ in water pressure after the shower was fixed.

10. The safety team _____ how to turn off the gas.

11. Our final exam covered chapters 1 _____ 8.

12. Dana thought she deserved a pay _____ after two years.

The president lives and works in the White House.

Exercise 5 What Do You Think?

Read each question and write a brief answer. Explain your answers in complete sentences.

1. What do you think is a major challenge for the president today?

   _____

   _____

   _____

2. Does an increase in high temperatures demonstrate global warming?

   _____

   _____

   _____

3. Is a manager effective if he or she regularly rejects suggestions?

   _____

   _____

   _____

Reading Connection

Read the following passage and answer the questions.

What Is the Temperature?

Can water freeze at two different temperatures? In a way, yes it can. The answer depends on which temperature scale you use.

In most of the world, water freezes at 0°C. That means 0 degrees on the Celsius scale. In some countries, however, water freezes at 32°F. That means 32 degrees on the Fahrenheit scale.

Most countries use the Celsius scale. The United States and a few other countries use the Fahrenheit scale to measure temperatures. In the United States, 38° is cold. However, in countries that use the Celsius scale, 38° is very hot!

The two different scales are named for the men who invented them. Daniel Gabriel Fahrenheit was born in 1686 in Germany. He was a scientist and became well known for making very good thermometers. His thermometer scale is divided into 212 degrees. Water boils at 212°F.

Anders Celsius was from Sweden. He was born there in 1701. He was an astronomer. He created his thermometer scale in 1742. His scale is divided into 100 degrees. Water boils at 100°C.

In 1948, most of the world changed from the Fahrenheit scale to the Celsius scale.

1. What do you expect to happen when the temperature of water increases to 100°C or 212°F?

   _____

   _____

2. What do you think is a major reason most of the world changed to the Celsius scale in 1948?

   _____

   _____

3. What would be a benefit to the United States if it rejected the Fahrenheit scale and used the Celsius scale? What would this demonstrate to the rest of the world?

   _____

   _____

4. Do you like to refer to a thermometer that uses the Celsius or the Fahrenheit scale?

   _____

   _____

benefit **demonstrate** adequate available
increase challenge benefit approval focus
option expect **major** consider demonstrate
decrease possess focus physical **reject**
quite adequate release **through** evaluate

New Word List

☐ demonstrate

☐ increase

☐ major

☐ reject

☐ through

Review Word List

☐ _____

☐ _____

☐ _____

☐ _____

☐ _____

Exercise 7 # Writing Connection

Write a brief response to each question. Use words from this lesson or previous lessons in your answer. Write your answers in complete sentences.

Cathy Benson's interview went well. The supervisor thought her interview demonstrated that she would be a good worker. Describe Cathy's interview. What did she do to demonstrate her qualities?

_____

_____

_____

_____

_____

What is your favorite major holiday? Why? What do you do to celebrate it?

_____

_____

_____

_____

_____

Exercise 8 # Reflection

Think about the words you have studied in this lesson.

1. Which words did you enjoy learning? _____

2. Select one word and imagine where you will use the word. Explain the situation.

   _____

   _____

3. Which words do you still need help with? _____

4. Return to the Knowledge Rating Chart at the beginning of this lesson. Complete column 3. How have your responses changed?

benefit demonstrate **adequate** available quite
increase challenge benefit **approval** focus
option expect **consider** major demonstrate
decrease possess focus physical reject
quite adequate release through **evaluate**

Vocabulary Knowledge Rating Chart

How well do you know the words? Use the numbers to rate your knowledge of the vocabulary words. Follow the teacher's directions.

4 = I know the word. I know it well enough to teach it to someone else.
3 = The word is familiar. I think I know what it means.
2 = I have heard the word, but I'm not sure what it means.
1 = I don't know the word at all.

	My rating before instruction	I think the word means	My rating after instruction
adequate			
approval			
consider			
decrease			
evaluate			

Word Meaning Chart

Complete the chart. Follow the teacher's directions.

adequate (adjective) /AD i kwit/

The word **adequate** means to have enough of something or that it is good enough.

EXAMPLES

The dark corner does not have _____ light for a plant to grow.

Class Example: _____

My Example: If I do not get **adequate** rest at night, _____

approval (noun) /uh PROO vuhl/   To give **approval** means you agree with an idea or action.

EXAMPLES

Tina received _____ from the landlord to paint her apartment.

Class Example: _____

My Example: Children need the **approval** of their parents to _____

consider (verb) /kuhn SID er/

To **consider** is to think very carefully before making a decision.

EXAMPLES

Schools need to _____ what is best for students.

Class Example: _____

My Example: Before I buy an expensive gift, I **consider** _____

decrease (verb) /dih KREES/

To **decrease** is to become smaller in size, number, or quantity.

EXAMPLES

Good diet and exercise _____ the risk of heart attacks.

Class Example: _____

My Example: I would like to **decrease** the time I spend _____

evaluate (verb) /ih VAL yoo eyt/   To **evaluate** is to judge how good or useful something is.

EXAMPLES

Teachers use tests as a way to _____ their students.

Class Example: _____

My Example: Doctors **evaluate** patients so they will know _____

Exercise 1   Use the Words

Complete each sentence. Write the correct form of the vocabulary word in the blank space.

1. Experts tell us to keep an _____ supply of food and water for emergencies.

2. Did the parent group give its _____ for the new playground?

3. Javier and Pamela are _____ a cruise to Alaska to celebrate their anniversary.

4. New car sales _____ when the economy is weak.

5. Health inspectors _____ restaurants to make sure they are clean.

Exercise 2   Complete the Sentences

These sentences have been started for you. They are not complete. Complete them with your own words.

1. At home I don't have adequate space for _____

_____

_____

2. A store clerk needs the approval of a supervisor to _____

_____

_____

3. When I select a cell phone plan, I consider _____

_____

_____

4. To create an ideal world, I would decrease _____

_____

_____

5. When I evaluate a teacher, I consider _____

_____

_____

Words at Work

Circle the best answer to each multiple choice question below. Then write a brief response to the question that follows. Write your answers in complete sentences.

---

1. Laila asked her manager for a day off to go to her daughter's graduation. The manager said she would consider it. Why?

   (A) She has to check the work schedule.

   (B) She does not like Laila.

   (C) She wants a day off too.

   What should an employee consider before taking a day off? _____

   _____

   _____

2. Ivan was asked to evaluate the quality of two different sewing machines. What did he do?

   (A) He tested both machines.

   (B) He took pictures of the machines.

   (C) He cleaned the machines.

   What have you been asked to evaluate at school or work? How did you do it? _____

   _____

   _____

3. Jason Yang is a plumber. He needs a car for school and work. He looked at a used car last week. He decided it was not adequate for his needs. What was his major reason?

   (A) The tires were old but adequate.

   (B) The seats were not adequate. They were torn and dirty.

   (C) There was not adequate space for his tools.

   What kind of car is adequate for your needs? _____

   _____

   _____

4. Doris is very busy. She has four children, works part time, and goes to school at night. What should she decrease to help make good use of her time?

   (A) the time she spends helping her children with homework

   (B) the number of meals she prepares for her family

   (C) the time she spends on the phone with friends

   What can you decrease to make more time in your schedule? _____

   _____

Word Families

Most words are part of a family of words. Study the word families on this page. Then fill in the missing words in the sentences below using the words from this lesson. Use the correct form of each word to complete the sentences.

---

adequate *(adjective)*

- **adequately** *(adverb)*
  Students who are adequately prepared for the test will do well.

approval *(noun)*

- **approve** *(verb)*
  The gas company approved a rate increase.

consider *(verb)*

- **consideration** *(noun)*
  Construction of a new high school is under consideration by the school board.

  Young people give careful consideration to the clothes they wear.

decrease *(verb)*

- **decrease** *(noun)*
  Cafeteria workers noticed a decrease in the sales of cheeseburgers.

evaluate *(verb)*

- **evaluation** *(noun)*
  Mr. Green gives a written evaluation to each worker on his project team.

---

1. Barbara worried that she was not _____ trained for her new job.

2. The crowd showed its _____ of the speaker's ideas with loud shouts.

3. The mayor's office did not _____ putting red-light cameras at busy intersections.

4. After careful _____, we decided to move.

5. The gym closed because of a _____ in its membership.

6. Who does the final _____ of the dancers?

7. The post office on Grand Avenue does not have _____ parking.

8. Steven _____ buying a new set of tools.

9. We need to _____ the new computer software before we buy it.

10. The attendance at the basketball game _____ by 20 percent last year.

An election campaign is an essential and expensive part of American politics.

Exercise 5 What Do You Think?

Read each question and write a brief answer. Explain your answers in complete sentences.

1. Should politicians consider ways to decrease campaign spending?

   _____

   _____

   _____

2. Some people take pills to decrease their appetite to lose weight. Do you approve? Why or why not?

   _____

   _____

   _____

3. Would it be difficult to evaluate the job performance of a friend?

   _____

   _____

   _____

Exercise 6 # Reading Connection

Read the following passage and answer the questions.

The Balance of Power in the U.S. Government

The leaders who wrote the United States Constitution had a concern. They worried that one person in government could have too much power. They created a government that had checks and balances. They divided the powers of the government into three branches. They are the executive branch, the legislative branch, and the judicial branch. Refer to the charts below to see the major powers given to each branch.

None of the branches has all of the powers. Each branch only has some powers. Each branch checks the power of the other two branches. For example, the legislative branch passes laws. However, the president must sign the laws. Sometimes a president does not sign a law if he thinks it is not effective.

The president selects the Supreme Court judges. Congress must approve the president's selections. The Supreme Court can say that a law violates the Constitution. Congress, however, has the power to change the Constitution.

Is it an ideal government? Some would say that it is not perfect. However, the authors of the Constitution thought dividing power would make a better government.

Executive Branch President Vice President Secretary of State Secretary of Defense other cabinet departments **Powers:** Enforce the laws Collect taxes Protect the country	**Legislative Branch** Congress Senate (100 members) House of Representatives (435 members) **Powers:** Make and pass laws Approve the budget	**Judicial Branch** The Supreme Court Federal Courts **Powers:** Decide the meaning of laws Decide if a law violates the Constitution

1. How does the president demonstrate his approval of a law that Congress passes?

_____

2. What is the purpose of the Supreme Court's evaluation of laws?

_____

_____

3. Consider the idea of checks and balances. Do you think it is an effective way to run a government?

_____

benefit demonstrate **adequate** available quite
increase challenge benefit **approval** focus
option expect **consider** major demonstrate
decrease possess focus physical reject
quite adequate release through **evaluate**

New Word List

☐ adequate

☐ approval

☐ consider

☐ decrease

☐ evaluate

Review Word List

☐ _____

☐ _____

☐ _____

☐ _____

☐ _____

Writing Connection

Write a brief response to each question. Use words from this lesson or previous lessons in your answer. Write your answers in complete sentences.

The children in the Taylor family want a pet. What things should a family consider before getting a pet? What items are needed for the adequate care of a pet?

_____

_____

_____

_____

Imagine you have been selected to be a judge for a contest. Is it for dance, sports, cooking, or something else? Describe the contest and how you are going to evaluate the participants.

_____

_____

_____

_____

Reflection

Think about the words you have studied in this lesson.

1. Which words did you enjoy learning? _____

2. Select one word and imagine where you will use the word. Explain the situation.

   _____

   _____

3. Which words do you still need help with? _____

4. Return to the Knowledge Rating Chart at the beginning of this lesson. Complete column 3. How have your responses changed?

benefit **available** demonstrate adequate quite

increase challenge **focus** benefit approval

expect consider major **option** demonstrate

decrease **possess** focus physical reject

adequate release through evaluate **quite**

Vocabulary Knowledge Rating Chart

How well do you know the words? Use the numbers to rate your knowledge of the vocabulary words. Follow the teacher's directions.

4 = I know the word. I know it well enough to teach it to someone else.
3 = The word is familiar. I think I know what it means.
2 = I have heard the word, but I'm not sure what it means.
1 = I don't know the word at all.

	My rating before instruction	I think the word means	My rating after instruction
available			
focus			
option			
possess			
quite			

Word Meaning Chart

Complete the chart. Follow the teacher's directions.

available *(adjective)* /uh VEY luh buhl/
Available means a person is free to do something or an item is able to be used or found.

EXAMPLES

Postage stamps are _____ online.

Class Example: _____

My Example: I am **available** to help my classmates _____

focus *(verb)* /FOH kuhs/
To **focus** means to put attention on one thing, idea, or person.

EXAMPLES

The president's speech _____ on the economy.

Class Example: _____

My Example: To **focus** my mind on something, I _____

option *(noun)* /OP shuhn/
An **option** is a choice.

EXAMPLES

Smoking is not an _____ on airplanes.

Class Example: _____

My Example: For my birthday, I would like the **option** of _____

possess *(verb)* /puh ZES/
To **possess** means to have or own something.

EXAMPLES

Museums _____ most of the world's great art.

Class Example: _____

My Example: People who **possess** a kind heart show it by _____

quite *(adverb)* /kwahyt/
The word **quite** means very or a lot.

EXAMPLES

It was _____ warm in the small room.

Class Example: _____

My Example: I am **quite** happy when _____

Exercise 1 Use the Words

Complete each sentence. Write the correct form of the vocabulary word in the blank space.

1. Super heroes _____ great powers and abilities.

2. Basketball players are usually _____ tall.

3. When will you be _____ to help with the painting?

4. You have the _____ of doing research during class or at the library.

5. The photographer _____ on the candidate's husband and children.

Exercise 2 Complete the Sentences

These sentences have been started for you. They are not complete. Complete them with your own words.

1. I was quite surprised when _____

_____

_____

2. One specific skill I possess is _____

_____

_____

_____

3. To meet my goal, I need to focus on _____

_____

_____

_____

4. A service I need that is not available at school is _____

_____

_____

5. We don't have a car today, so our options are _____

_____

_____

Words at Work

Circle the best answer to each multiple choice question below. Then write a brief response to the question that follows. Write your answers in complete sentences.

1. Rod has tickets to go to a concert with a friend. He wants to leave at 4:45 p.m. However, his supervisor tells him he can't leave early because his work is not finished. What is Rod's best option?

   (A) leave work at 4:30   **(B)** call his friend to cancel   **(C)** ask to come in early the next day to finish the work

   At the end of the day, what do you do when you have not finished your work? _____

   _____

   _____

2. Ms. Lopez interviewed Johann for a secretarial job. She thought he possessed good job skills for the position. What did Ms. Lopez mean?

   (A) He smiled and wore a tie.   **(B)** He knew how to use several computer programs.   **(C)** He turned off his cellphone.

   What job skills do you possess or would you like to possess? _____

   _____

   _____

3. Ed's attention was not focused on driving. He was talking to his wife on the cell phone. The radio was playing too. What happened?

   (A) He couldn't hear his wife.   **(B)** The light turned green.   **(C)** He almost had an accident.

   Why is it important for a driver to focus while driving? What specific things can drivers do?

   _____

   _____

4. Kit is available to go to school after work. She works until 4:30 p.m. on Monday, Tuesday, and Friday. She works until 5:00 p.m. on Wednesday and Thursday. Which class can she take?

   (A) Math: Mon. & Wed., 3:30-5:30 p.m.   **(B)** English: Tues. & Thurs., 4:00-6:00 p.m.   **(C)** Computer: Thurs., 6:00-9:30 p.m.

   What classes would you like to be available at your school? _____

   _____

   _____

Word Families

Most words are part of a family of words. Study the word families on this page. Then fill in the missing words in the sentences below using the words from this lesson. Use the correct form of each word to complete the sentences.

---

available *(adjective)*

- availability *(noun)*
  Many people want the government to increase the availability of health care.

possess *(verb)*

- possession *(noun)*
  The gold necklace was my aunt's favorite possession.

option *(noun)*

- optional *(adjective)*
  Leather seats are optional in a new car.

focus *(verb)*

- focus *(noun)*
  The focus of the article was on recycling plastic.
- focused *(adjective)*
  Arnold is very focused on learning to play the guitar.

quite *(adverb)*

- quite a few *(idiom)*
  The room was crowded because there were quite a few people at the party. (countable)
- quite a bit *(idiom)*
  There was quite a bit of food left after the party. (non-countable)
- not quite *(idiom)*
  The cake is not quite done baking. It needs five more minutes.

---

1. Are jackets and ties required or _____ ?

2. The old watch is one of the man's favorite _____ .

3. _____ people are on the waiting list for the computer class.

4. We need to check the _____ of flights before we make plans.

5. The party was _____ noisy, so they left early.

6. Mr. Escalante _____ a high school diploma from Bolivia.

7. I think we made too much spaghetti because there is _____ left.

8. Don't forget you have the _____ of paying the bill online.

9. Are strawberries _____ in winter?

10. Everyone's eyes _____ on the bride as she walked down the aisle.

11. The painters have _____ finished. They will be back tomorrow.

Parents and school officials worry about the eating habits of children at school.

Exercise 5 What Do You Think?

Read each question and write a brief answer. Explain your answers in complete sentences.

1. Should foods with quite a bit of sugar be available to children at school?

_____

_____

_____

2. Should everyone have the option to possess a driver's license?

_____

_____

_____

3. Is it better to possess good health or a lot of money?

_____

_____

_____

Reading Connection

Read the following passage and answer the questions.

What Is Jazz?

What do you know about jazz music? Have you ever heard it? Do you know where it started? Have you listened to any of the major jazz artists? Louis Armstrong, Billie Holiday, Miles Davis, Ella Fitzgerald, and Wynton Marsalis are some of the most famous jazz artists.

People all over the world love jazz. However, jazz started in the United States about 100 years ago. It started in the Southern city of New Orleans. It is a specifically American form of music.

African-Americans who lived in New Orleans in the early 1900s had a rich tradition of music. This music had its roots in the slave experience. There were also people in New Orleans from Africa, Europe, the Caribbean, Latin America, and other parts of the world. These people brought their music with them too. Over the years, the different types of music started to mix together.

Jazz was born from the mix of these different kinds of music. Early jazz was mostly for dancing. Later, people would sit and listen to it.

Many people love jazz. The music has strong rhythms that make people feel good and want to dance. The music can express different feelings to different people—pain and sadness, or joy and happiness.

An essential part of jazz is something called improvisation. That is when an artist makes up the music along the way without a plan. Jazz artists like to have their own style of playing. Improvisation is a good way to show style.

Jazz is as popular today as ever.

1. What was a major reason jazz started in New Orleans?

   _____

   _____

2. Why must a jazz artist be focused to be good at improvisation?

   _____

   _____

3. Jazz is an American form of music. However, jazz is quite popular all over the world. What could be a reason for that?

   _____

   _____

benefit **available** demonstrate adequate quite
increase challenge **focus** benefit approval
expect consider major **option** demonstrate
decrease **possess** focus physical reject
adequate release through evaluate **quite**

New Word List

☐ available

☐ focus

☐ option

☐ possess

☐ quite

Review Word List

☐ _____

☐ _____

☐ _____

☐ _____

☐ _____

Writing Connection

Write a brief response to each question. Use words from this lesson or previous lessons in your answer. Write your answers in complete sentences.

Reflect on a special possession. Describe it. Why do you consider it special?

_____

_____

_____

_____

_____

Your friend Janet is quite stressed because she has so much to do. Her husband got a promotion. They are moving to another city. She has to sell their condo, find a new place to live, quit her job, and find another job. Give Janet some advice to help her focus on her tasks.

_____

_____

_____

_____

_____

Reflection

Think about the words you have studied in this lesson.

1. Which words did you enjoy learning? _____

2. Select one word and imagine where you will use the word. Explain the situation.

_____

_____

3. Which words do you still need help with? _____

4. Return to the Knowledge Rating Chart at the beginning of this lesson. Complete column 3. How have your responses changed?

Activity 1 Ask Questions

Look at the picture. Imagine you have the opportunity to ask these people about their journey. Write at least five questions you want to ask them. Use one or more of the vocabulary words you have studied in this unit in each question. You may also use words from previous units. Underline each vocabulary word you use. Some of your questions can begin with *Who, What, When, Where, Why,* or *How.*

Example: What do you <u>consider</u> the biggest <u>challenge</u> of your trip?

_____

_____

_____

_____

_____

_____

_____

_____

_____

_____

_____

WORD BANK

ADEQUATE
APPROVAL
AVAILABLE
BENEFIT
CHALLENGE
CONSIDER
DECREASE
DEMONSTRATE
EVALUATE
EXPECT
FOCUS
INCREASE
MAJOR
OPTION
PHYSICAL
POSSESS
QUITE
REJECT
RELEASE
THROUGH

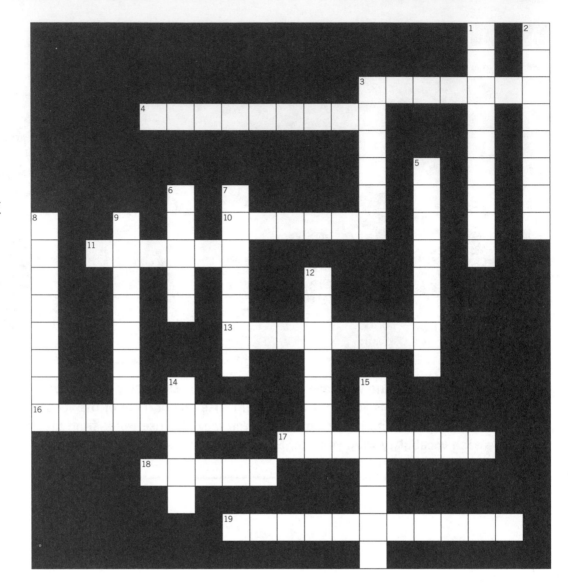

Activity 2 Puzzle

ACROSS

3. The hospital won't _____ the names of those in the accident.
4. Parking is _____ behind the building.
10. We _____ to finish the job next week.
11. You have the _____ of canceling your membership.
13. An _____ in taxes is always unpopular.
16. The players were asked to _____ their coach.
17. I need more _____ exercise.
18. Immigration was the _____ of the senator's speech.
19. Who can _____ how to use the new camera?

DOWN

1. Learning another language is a _____.
2. The room didn't have _____ light to read.
3. Why did the machine _____ my card?
5. Please _____ making a donation.
6. We were _____ tired, so we left early.
7. What's the _____ of taking this class?
8. We want a _____ in the price of gas.
9. Children need the _____ of parents to go on school trips.
12. It took an hour to get _____ the line.
14. The mall has two _____ department stores.
15. Do you _____ a driver's license?

Activity 3   Synonyms

Complete these sentences. Use the correct form of the vocabulary word that means the same as the word in parentheses.

Example: When the bird gets better, we will _____ *release* _____ (*free*) it into the forest.

1. I have the _____ (*choice*) of taking the bus or driving to work.

2. Does the applicant _____ (*have*) a high school diploma?

3. The chef _____ (*showed*) how to barbecue a chicken.

Activity 4   Antonyms

Complete these sentences. Use the correct form of the vocabulary word that means the opposite of the word in parentheses.

Example: It is a _____ *major* _____ (*small*) challenge to find good child care.

1. Riding a bicycle is _____ (*mental*) exercise.

2. Maggie _____ (*accepted*) her sister's advice to decrease her work hours.

3. Are you _____ (*busy*) next Saturday to work for me?

Activity 5   Practice Grammar with New Vocabulary

Rewrite the sentences. Change the <u>underlined</u> word or words from singular to plural. Change other words from singular to plural as necessary.

Example: Has <u>Mr. Binh</u> ever considered increasing the size of his office?
Have Mr. and Mrs. Binh ever considered increasing the size of their office?

1. <u>This room</u> is available, and it has adequate space.

_____

2. Why was Mrs. Johnson's <u>child</u> released from her class?

_____

3. Every spring, the <u>teacher</u> evaluates herself and reflects on her job.

_____

4. Does <u>John</u> expect to get his manager's approval for his project soon?

_____

Unit 3

minimum
convince
provide
familiar
expand
moreover
definite
accurate
destroy
obvious
universal
fundamental
damage
prevent
amount
confirm
reveal
reinforce
issue
maximum

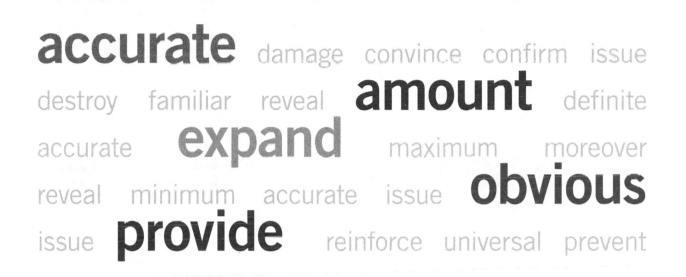

accurate damage convince confirm issue
destroy familiar reveal **amount** definite
accurate **expand** maximum moreover
reveal minimum accurate issue **obvious**
issue **provide** reinforce universal prevent

Vocabulary Knowledge Rating Chart

How well do you know the words? Use the numbers to rate your knowledge of the vocabulary words. Follow the teacher's directions.

4 = I know the word. I know it well enough to teach it to someone else.
3 = The word is familiar. I think I know what it means.
2 = I have heard the word, but I'm not sure what it means.
1 = I don't know the word at all.

	My rating before instruction	I think the word means	My rating after instruction
accurate			
amount			
expand			
obvious			
provide			

Word Meaning Chart

Complete the chart. Follow the teacher's directions.

accurate (adjective) /AK yer it/ — Accurate means that something is correct.

EXAMPLES

I never miss the bus because my watch is _____.

Class Example: _____

My Example: It is important for me to be **accurate** when _____

amount (noun) /uh MOUNT/ — Amount means a quantity of something.

EXAMPLES

What is an ideal _____ of money to have?

Class Example: _____

My Example: A large **amount** of my time is spent _____

expand (verb) /ik SPAND/ — To expand means to become larger.

EXAMPLES

A balloon _____ when it is filled with air.

Class Example: _____

My Example: To **expand** my circle of friends, I can _____

obvious (adjective) /OB vee uhs/ — Obvious means easy to see or understand.

EXAMPLES

An _____ place to hide your key is under the doormat.

Class Example: _____

My Example: It was **obvious** the student was excited because _____

provide (verb) /pruh VAHYD/ — To provide is to give something or to make it available.

EXAMPLES

Parents _____ food, clothing, and many other things to their children.

Class Example: _____

My Example: For me, this class **provides** _____

Use the Words

Complete each sentence. Write the correct form of the vocabulary word in the blank space.

1. The history book stated that Columbus sailed to America in 1992. That is an

   _____ mistake.

2. The coffee shop on the corner _____ free Internet access for
   customers.

3. We got lost because the directions were not _____.

4. Mrs. Lozzo used a small _____ of water to cook the vegetables.

5. The city wants to _____ its services for people with special needs.

Exercise 2 # Complete the Sentences

**These sentences have been started for you. They are not complete. Complete them with your
own words.**

1. It takes a large amount of _____ to _____

   _____

   _____

2. The library in my community is important because it provides _____

   _____

   _____

3. If a carpenter is not accurate, _____

   _____

   _____

4. It is obvious that children in the United States _____

   _____

   _____

5. To expand my knowledge of the city's neighborhoods, I can _____

   _____

   _____

Words at Work

Circle the best answer to each multiple choice question below. Then write a brief response to the question that follows. Write your answers in complete sentences.

---

1. The nurse weighed Tyrone on the scale at the doctor's office. The result was an obvious surprise to him. He asked the nurse, "Are you sure this scale is accurate?" Why was Tyrone surprised?

   (A) He weighed more than he thought.

   (B) He weighed exactly what he thought.

   (C) It was his first time on a scale.

   What equipment or machines do you use that must be accurate? How do you know if they are

   accurate? _____

   _____

   _____

2. Sonia has a small restaurant in her neighborhood. She wants to expand the services she provides to her customers. What will she need to do?

   (A) order more menus

   (B) open for breakfast

   (C) increase the prices

   What services would you like your school or work to expand? Be specific. _____

   _____

   _____

3. Benjamin is a gardener. He is quite happy to work in Mrs. Robinson's yard. Why?

   (A) He provides his own tools.

   (B) She provides water and lunch.

   (C) She provides books and magazines.

   What would you like a workplace to provide for you? Be specific. _____

   _____

   _____

4. Rita was happy to return to work after a brief vacation. However, the amount of work for Rita and her coworkers had increased. Why?

   (A) The company expanded the number of employees.

   (B) The company decreased the number of employees.

   (C) The company decreased the amount of time for lunch.

   What do you do when there is an increase in your amount of work? _____

   _____

   _____

Word Families

Most words are part of a family of words. Study the word families on this page. Then fill in the missing words in the sentences below using the words from this lesson. Use the correct form of each word to complete the sentences.

---

accurate *(adjective)*

- accuracy *(noun)*
  Danna does her work with speed and accuracy.

- accurately *(adverb)*
  Melissa accurately described the robber to the police.

expand *(verb)*

- expansion *(noun)*
  The hospital is planning an expansion of its children's section.

obvious *(adjective)*

- obviously *(adverb)*
  Barry is obviously tired because he is falling asleep at his desk.

provide *(verb)*

- provider *(noun)*
  The Red Cross is a major provider of food and shelter for people in emergencies.

---

1. Did the film _____ tell the story of the famous athlete?

2. The roads were icy and _____ dangerous to drive on.

3. The _____ of the cafeteria will provide more room for tables.

4. New employees were offered insurance from the company's healthcare

   _____ .

5. It is _____ that the grass needs to be watered because it is getting brown.

6. Sunshine Bank wants to _____ its business in the county.

7. It is a good idea to question the _____ of things you read on the Internet.

8. The new drug _____ hope for people with diabetes.

9. The census report must be as _____ as possible.

10. The _____ of the park will include a new soccer field.

11. Is it possible to _____ predict the weather?

12. It was _____ Emily's dog because it came when she called its name.

Disaster relief stations provide people a great amount of help.

Exercise 5 What Do You Think?

Read each question and write a brief answer. Explain your answers in complete sentences.

1. Is there a limit to the amount of food and medicine we should provide to countries that experience a natural disaster?

_____

_____

_____

2. Would it be better to expand or decrease the amount of homework that American students have?

_____

_____

_____

3. Which sport requires more accuracy—baseball or soccer?

_____

_____

_____

Reading Connection

Inside the Supreme Court

The Supreme Court is the head of the judicial branch of government. It is the most important court in the country. Its purpose is to decide what laws mean and whether any laws violate the U.S. Constitution.

There are nine judges on the Supreme Court. There is one Chief Justice and eight Associate Justices. These men and women examine legal questions that are important to the nation.

The justices wear black robes and sit in tall leather chairs. A red curtain hangs behind them. Lawyers come to the Supreme Court to argue important court cases. The justices listen and ask questions. They study similar previous cases. Then they make a decision. Their decisions can lead to significant changes in the United States.

The Supreme Court made one of its most important decisions in 1954. At that time, black children in many parts of the country were forced to go to different schools than white children. The Supreme Court said it was against the Constitution to have separate public schools based on race. The decision helped to change American society. Schools became integrated. People began to consider the importance of equality in America.

1. What is the purpose of the Supreme Court?

_____

_____

_____

2. How did the Supreme Court expand the rights of black children in the United States?

_____

_____

_____

3. Why do Supreme Court justices expect lawyers to provide them with accurate information?

_____

_____

_____

accurate damage convince confirm issue
destroy familiar reveal **amount** definite
accurate **expand** maximum moreover
reveal minimum accurate issue **obvious**
issue **provide** reinforce universal prevent

New Word List

☐ accurate

☐ amount

☐ expand

☐ obvious

☐ provide

Review Word List

☐ _____

☐ _____

☐ _____

☐ _____

☐ _____

Exercise 7 Writing Connection

Write a brief response to each question. Use words from this lesson or previous lessons in your answer. Write your answers in complete sentences.

What does it mean to "expand your mind?" How does a person expand his or her mind? Give at least two examples.

_____

_____

_____

_____

_____

Choose a person who provides an obviously good example for people. Describe two or three ways he or she provides a good example.

_____

_____

_____

_____

_____

Exercise 8 Reflection

Think about the words you have studied in this lesson.

1. Which words did you enjoy learning? _____

2. Select one word and imagine where you will use the word. Explain the situation.

_____

_____

3. Which words do you still need help with? _____

4. Return to the Knowledge Rating Chart at the beginning of this lesson. Complete column 3. How have your responses changed?

accurate **damage** convince confirm issue
destroy familiar reveal amount definite
fundamental expand **maximum** moreover
reveal **minimum** accurate issue obvious
issue reinforce universal provide **prevent**

Vocabulary Knowledge Rating Chart

How well do you know the words? Use the numbers to rate your knowledge of the vocabulary words. Follow the teacher's directions.

4 = I know the word. I know it well enough to teach it to someone else.
3 = The word is familiar. I think I know what it means.
2 = I have heard the word, but I'm not sure what it means.
1 = I don't know the word at all.

	My rating before instruction	I think the word means	My rating after instruction
damage			
destroy			
maximum			
minimum			
prevent			

Word Meaning Chart

Complete the chart. Follow the teacher's directions.

damage *(noun)* /DAM ij/
Damage is the harm that is done to something.

EXAMPLES

The _____ from the hurricane will cost millions of dollars.

Class Example: _____

My Example: **Damage** may be caused to computers by _____

destroy *(verb)* /dih STROI/
To **destroy** means to damage something so it cannot be used or does not exist.

EXAMPLES

The flood water _____ the furniture on the first floor of our house.

Class Example: _____

My Example: Fires can **destroy** _____

maximum *(adjective)* /MAK suh muhm/
Maximum means the greatest amount or size possible.

EXAMPLES

The _____ speed limit on most city streets is 35 miles per hour.

Class Example: _____

My Example: The **maximum** amount I would spend on a movie ticket is _____

minimum *(adjective)* /MIN uh muhm/
Minimum means the smallest amount or size possible.

EXAMPLES

The _____ age to be president of the United States is 35.

Class Example: _____

My Example: One thing I can do with a **minimum** amount of difficulty is _____

prevent *(verb)* /pri VENT/
To **prevent** is to stop something from happening.

EXAMPLES

Seat belts _____ people from getting seriously hurt in car accidents.

Class Example: _____

My Example: The best way to **prevent** getting sick is _____

Exercise 1 Use the Words

Complete each sentence. Write the correct form of the vocabulary word in the blank space.

1. Too much sun can cause skin _____.

2. The _____ weight for one suitcase on an airplane is 50 pounds.

3. A broken ankle _____ Arlene from playing volleyball at the beach.

4. The senator's unpopular decisions _____ his career.

5. Do you think that the _____ wage should be increased?

Exercise 2 Complete the Sentences

These sentences have been started for you. They are not complete. Complete them with your own words.

1. There is a minimum age to get a driver's license because _____

   _____

   _____

2. My community can prevent more crimes if we _____

   _____

   _____

3. The maximum amount of time I can spend at the beach today is one hour because _____

   _____

   _____

4. After the storm the family discovered damage to _____

   _____

   _____

5. His chances for a promotion were destroyed because _____

   _____

   _____

Words at Work

Circle the best answer to each multiple choice question below. Then write a brief response to the question that follows. Write your answers in complete sentences.

---

1. Dave accidentally put the wrong kind of paper in the copy machine. The paper damaged the machine. Dave's manager was quite upset. The manager should

   (A) buy more paper.   **(B)** put Dave on probation.   **(C)** post a notice to remind people about the copier.

   At home or at work, what do you have to use carefully to prevent damage? _____

   _____

   _____

2. Manny works at a nursery. He noticed that a customer's dog destroyed several small plants. The customer did not pay for them. What should Manny do?

   (A) call the police   **(B)** call the customer at home   **(C)** tell the owner of the nursery what he saw

   If you noticed someone destroying plants or other property, what would you do? _____

   _____

   _____

3. Josie received her credit card bill. She has the option to pay the maximum amount of the bill or the minimum amount due. If she pays the maximum amount, she pays

   (A) 100% of the bill.   **(B)** 50% of the bill.   **(C)** 25% of the bill.

   What is the benefit of paying the maximum amount of a credit card bill? _____

   _____

   _____

4. A company rule prevents employees from taking gifts from customers. One of Joe's customers gave him a $10 gift card. Should he keep the gift card?

   (A) Yes, because nobody will know.   **(B)** Yes, because $10 is a small amount.   **(C)** No, because it is a gift.

   Describe a rule or policy at school or work that prevents you from doing something. _____

   _____

   _____

   _____

Word Families

Most words are part of a family of words. Study the word families on this page. Then fill in the missing words in the sentences below using the words from this lesson. Use the correct form of each word to complete the sentences.

---

damage *(noun)*

- damage *(verb)*
  Smoking damages a person's lungs and other organs.

destroy *(verb)*

- destruction *(noun)*
  Many organizations work to stop the destruction of the tropical rain forests.

- destructive *(adjective)*
  The destructive force of a tornado is obvious when you see the damage.

maximum *(adjective)*

- maximum *(noun)*
  The elevator can hold a maximum of 10 people at one time.

minimum *(adjective)*

- minimum *(noun)*
  Credit cards require you to pay a minimum on your account every month.

prevent *(verb)*

- prevention *(noun)*
  The prevention of HIV/AIDS is still a major challenge in the world.

- preventable *(adjective)*
  Sunburn is preventable if you use sunscreen.

---

1. I _____ my car quite a bit when I hit the wall.

2. The express line at the grocery store has a _____ of 15 items.

3. If you want to use your credit card, there is a ten-dollar _____.

4. Was there major _____ when the water pipe broke?

5. Is it possible to _____ children from making noise?

6. The dentist told her that the _____ of tooth decay is important.

7. The radio was turned up to the _____ volume.

8. A new puppy may become _____ when left alone.

9. The guitar class needs a _____ of five students, or it will close.

10. Did you _____ those old letters and papers before you moved?

11. The complete _____ of the old stadium took several weeks.

Team sports teach children about the benefits of physical activity.

Exercise 5 What Do You Think?

Read each question and write a brief answer. Explain your answers in complete sentences.

1. Do you need a minimum amount of experience with children to be an effective coach?

2. Should there be a maximum age for people to drive? Should older people be prevented from driving when they reach a maximum age?

3. Do you think parents are responsible when their children damage public property?

Reading Connection

Read the following passage and answer the questions.

When the Earth Moves

Have you ever felt the earth move? If you have, you know an earthquake is a scary experience. Scientists think that earthquakes happen about 8,000 times every day. That means right now, somewhere in the world, the earth is moving! Most earthquakes are too small for us to feel and do not cause any damage.

What is an earthquake? What causes it? An earthquake happens when a section of rock deep inside the earth moves. This movement causes the ground to shake.

The inside of the earth has different layers of rock. The layer that is close to the surface, or top, is called the crust. The earth's crust is made up of different sections. These sections are called plates. The plates are always moving. Sometimes one plate gets stuck against another plate, and they become locked together. Plates can stay locked for hundreds or thousands of years. Eventually, they will move. The plates release energy when they move. The shaking we feel is the energy moving through the earth when the plates move. That's an earthquake!

A major earthquake releases a great amount of energy. The shaking is very strong. A major earthquake can destroy buildings, bridges, and highways. It can cause parts of the earth's surface to move.

Earthquakes happen in most parts of the world. However, some parts of the world have more earthquakes than other places. For example, the South American country Chile has had many major earthquakes. One of the strongest earthquakes in the world happened in Alaska in 1964.

1. What happens inside the earth during an earthquake?

   _____

   _____

2. A major earthquake can destroy things and cause great physical damage. What kinds of challenges do people experience because of the destruction?

   _____

   _____

   _____

3. How can people adequately prepare for an earthquake or other disasters? What are some essential things they can do?

   _____

   _____

   _____

accurate **damage** convince confirm issue
destroy familiar reveal amount definite
fundamental expand **maximum** moreover
reveal **minimum** accurate issue obvious
issue reinforce universal provide **prevent**

New Word List

☐ damage

☐ destroy

☐ maximum

☐ minimum

☐ prevent

Review Word List

☐ _____

☐ _____

☐ _____

☐ _____

☐ _____

Exercise 7 # Writing Connection

Write a brief response to each question. Use words from this lesson or previous lessons in your answer. Write your answers in complete sentences.

Benjamin Franklin was a wise man. He once said, "An ounce of prevention is worth a pound of cure." Consider what Franklin said. What do you think he meant? Give an example.

_____

_____

_____

_____

_____

Sometimes people cause damage in their friendships or other relationships. Is it always possible to fix the damage? Reflect on your own experience and give an example.

_____

_____

_____

_____

_____

Exercise 8 # Reflection

Think about the words you have studied in this lesson.

1. Which words did you enjoy learning? _____

2. Select one word and imagine where you will use the word. Explain the situation.

_____

_____

3. Which words do you still need help with? _____

4. Return to the Knowledge Rating Chart at the beginning of this lesson. Complete column 3. How have your responses changed?

accurate damage **convince** confirm issue
destroy familiar reveal amount **definite**
fundamental expand maximum reveal
confirm minimum accurate **issue** obvious
issue **reinforce** universal provide prevent

Vocabulary Knowledge Rating Chart

How well do you know the words? Use the numbers to rate your knowledge of the vocabulary words. Follow the teacher's directions.

4 = I know the word. I know it well enough to teach it to someone else.
3 = The word is familiar. I think I know what it means.
2 = I have heard the word, but I'm not sure what it means.
1 = I don't know the word at all.

	My rating before instruction	I think the word means	My rating after instruction
convince			
definite			
fundamental			
issue			
reinforce			

Word Meaning Chart

Complete the chart. Follow the teacher's directions.

convince *(verb)* /kuhn VINS/

To **convince** is to make someone believe something is true or necessary.

EXAMPLES

A candidate must _____ people to vote for her.

Class Example: _____

My Example: One way to **convince** young people to stay in school is _____

definite *(adjective)* /DEF uh nit/

Definite means clear and certain.

EXAMPLES

Marshall and Sue have a _____ date for the wedding.

Class Example: _____

My Example: I have **definite** plans next weekend to _____

fundamental *(adjective)* /fuhn duh MEN tl/

Fundamental means the most essential.

EXAMPLES

Reading and writing are _____ skills.

Class Example: _____

My Example: In soccer, a **fundamental** skill is _____

issue *(noun)* /ISH yoo/

An **issue** is an important topic or problem.

EXAMPLES

The students selected the _____ of homelessness for a class discussion.

Class Example: _____

My Example: An important **issue** for the president to consider is _____

reinforce *(verb)* /ree in FOHRS/

To **reinforce** something is to make it stronger.

EXAMPLES

Road workers used steel and concrete to _____ the highway overpass.

Class Example: _____

My Example: I can **reinforce** my computer skills by _____

Exercise 1   Use the Words

Complete each sentence. Write the correct form of the vocabulary word in the blank space.

1. Diabetes is a major health _____ for people today.

2. The lawyer _____ her argument with facts.

3. How did Sandra _____ her husband to buy new furniture?

4. Hunger is a _____ problem in many parts of the world.

5. Have Leon and Linda made a _____ decision to move?

Exercise 2   Complete the Sentences

These sentences have been started for you. They are not complete. Complete them with your own words.

1. An issue I feel quite strongly about is _____

   _____

   _____

2. A fundamental reason to change jobs is _____

   _____

   _____

   _____

3. It would be a challenge to convince me that _____

   _____

   _____

4. A definite benefit of having a cell phone is _____

   _____

   _____

5. Parents can reinforce good behavior in their children by _____

   _____

   _____

Exercise 3 Words at Work

Circle the best answer to each multiple choice question below. Then write a brief response to the question that follows. Write your answers in complete sentences.

1. Mr. Mack performs a fundamental task at work every morning. What does he do?

   (A) He turns on the radio.   **(B)** He reads the newspaper.   **(C)** He unlocks the doors.

   What is a fundamental task you perform at home or at work? _____

   _____

   _____

2. Adela wants to discuss the issue of child care at the next staff meeting. She wants to convince the staff that providing child care will

   (A) prevent employee   **(B)** increase employee   **(C)** demonstrate employee
   absences.   absences.   absences.

   What is an issue at school or work that is important to you? Explain. _____

   _____

   _____

3. Mark noticed that Byron took a heavy work manual home on the weekend. Mark asked Byron why. What was Byron's answer?

   (A) "I don't have definite   **(B)** "I want to reinforce my   **(C)** "I don't have room for it on
   plans this weekend."   understanding of my job."   my desk."

   How have you used a manual at work? How does a manual reinforce your understanding

   of your job? _____

   _____

   _____

4. Tammy's coworker Karen is trying to convince her to join a gym. Tammy does not have enough money for a gym membership. What can Tammy do?

   (A) talk to her manager   **(B)** buy a three-month   **(C)** thank Karen and explain
                                             membership   that it isn't a good time

   What are some things that your friends or coworkers try to convince you to do? _____

   _____

   _____

   _____

Exercise 4 # Word Families

Most words are part of a family of words. Study the word families on this page. Then fill in the missing words in the sentences below using the words from this lesson. Use the correct form of each word to complete the sentences.

---

convince (verb)
• convinced (adjective) I am quite convinced that selling the house is the right thing to do. • convincing (adjective) Mr. Tran made a convincing argument to expand the business.

definite (adjective)
• definitely (adverb) We will definitely meet you after work on Friday.

fundamental (adjective)
• fundamentally (adverb) Men and women are fundamentally different.

reinforce (verb)
• reinforcement (noun) Many old buildings need reinforcement to prevent earthquake damage. • reinforcements (noun-plural) The Army sent reinforcements to protect the city after the flood.

---

1. Dr. Nader's nurse says the doctor can _____ see patients all next week.

2. Marguerite could not provide a _____ explanation for the missing guitar.

3. Police _____ were needed to provide extra security.

4. Were the ancient Greeks _____ that the world was round?

5. It is not _____ that the hall will be available to rent.

6. There are a few problems with our emergency plan, but _____ it is good.

7. Ming's teacher gave her positive _____ during the project.

8. The long line of customers _____ us it was a good restaurant.

9. Basic math is an important _____ skill for many jobs.

10. What kind of practice helps _____ football skills?

11. It took several calls to the insurance company for Jill to get a

_____ answer to her question.

Technology makes information available to people all over the world.

Exercise 5 What Do You Think?

Read each question and write a brief answer. Explain your answers in complete sentences.

1. Do people have a fundamental right to all information available on the Internet?

_____

_____

_____

2. Is immigration a fundamental issue that everyone in the country should consider?

_____

_____

_____

3. Which person is easier to convince to vote in an election: a person who has definite opinions about issues or a person who doesn't have an opinion?

_____

_____

_____

Reading Connection

Read the following passage and answer the questions.

The United Nations

World War II ended in 1945. The damage and destruction after six years of war were huge. Over fifty million people were killed.

In June 1945, however, 50 countries came together in San Francisco. The purpose was to consider how to prevent war and make the world a better and safer place. These nations formed an international organization we know today as the United Nations, or the UN.

The work of the UN focuses on four major areas:

  1. international peace and security
  2. friendship among nations
  3. better living conditions around the world
  4. human rights

UN projects are found in many countries around the world. UN troops help keep the peace in places like Afghanistan, Indonesia, and Palestine. UN workers provide medicine and care to people in need in Africa, Asia, and other parts of the world. The UN also helps people after a disaster, such as an earthquake.

Many women and children benefit from the work of the UN. Have you heard of UNICEF—the United Nations International Children's Emergency Fund? UNICEF provides clean water, food, and medicine to families around the world.

The main office of the UN is located in New York City. Today, the UN has 192 members. The UN has six official languages. They are Arabic, Chinese, English, French, Russian, and Spanish. The UN also has its own flag, post office, and postage stamps. The official emblem, or symbol, of the UN shows the world held in olive branches. Olive branches are a symbol of peace.

More information about the United Nations is available at its web site. Go to www.un.org.

1. What was the purpose of the meeting in San Francisco in 1945?

    _____

    _____

2. On what fundamental issues does the UN focus?

    _____

    _____

3. How can countries reinforce the work of the UN?

    _____

    _____

accurate damage **convince** confirm issue
destroy familiar reveal amount **definite**
fundamental expand maximum reveal
confirm minimum accurate **issue** obvious
issue **reinforce** universal provide prevent

New Word List

☐ convince

☐ definite

☐ fundamental

☐ issue

☐ reinforce

Review Word List

☐ _____

☐ _____

☐ _____

☐ _____

☐ _____

| Exercise 7 | ## Writing Connection |

Write a brief response to each question. Use words from this lesson or previous lessons in your answer. Write your answers in complete sentences.

Select a specific issue that is important to you. Explain what the issue is and why it is important.

_____

_____

_____

_____

_____

You and your neighbors want to write a letter to the city about the definite need for streetlights in your neighborhood. Write down two or three reasons for the new streetlights. Reinforce your ideas with specific examples.

_____

_____

_____

_____

_____

| Exercise 8 | ## Reflection |

Think about the words you have studied in this lesson.

1. Which words did you enjoy learning? _____

2. Select one word and imagine where you will use the word. Explain the situation.

_____

_____

3. Which words do you still need help with? _____

4. Return to the Knowledge Rating Chart at the beginning of this lesson. Complete column 3. How have your responses changed?

accurate damage convince **confirm** issue

destroy **familiar** reveal amount definite

fundamental expand maximum **moreover**

reveal minimum accurate issue obvious

issue reinforce **universal** provide prevent

Vocabulary Knowledge Rating Chart

How well do you know the words? Use the numbers to rate your knowledge of the vocabulary words. Follow the teacher's directions.

4 = I know the word. I know it well enough to teach it to someone else.
3 = The word is familiar. I think I know what it means.
2 = I have heard the word, but I'm not sure what it means.
1 = I don't know the word at all.

	My rating before instruction	I think the word means	My rating after instruction
confirm			
familiar			
moreover			
reveal			
universal			

Word Meaning Chart

Complete the chart. Follow the teacher's directions.

confirm *(verb)* /kuhn FURM/
To **confirm** is to make sure that something is true or definite.

EXAMPLES

You can refer to the dictionary to _____ the spelling of a word.

Class Example: _____

My Example: If I need to **confirm** the school's address, I can _____

familiar *(adjective)* /fuh MIL yer/
Familiar means that you know something or someone from an earlier time.

EXAMPLES

She looks _____ to me. Was she in my English class?

Class Example: _____

My Example: That song sounds **familiar**. I think I heard it _____

moreover *(adverb)* /mohr OH ver/
Moreover means in addition.

EXAMPLES

Giving blood is simple and painless. _____, it can save a life.

Class Example: _____

My Example: Exercise can be fun. **Moreover**, it _____

reveal *(verb)* /ri VEEL/
To **reveal** is to show what was not seen or known before.

EXAMPLES

The lion opened its mouth to _____ huge, sharp teeth.

Class Example: _____

My Example: An x-ray of Doug's leg **revealed** that _____

universal *(adjective)* /yoo nuh VUR suhl/
Universal means common to everyone or available everywhere.

EXAMPLES

The color red is a _____ sign to stop.

Class Example: _____

My Example: Human beings have a **universal** right to _____

Use the Words

Complete each sentence. Write the correct form of the vocabulary word in the blank space.

1. Some people say that music is a _____ language.

2. Is there someone who can _____ your work experience?

3. Mexico City is an interesting city. _____, it is one of the oldest cities in North America.

4. Fred was _____ with the downtown area because he worked there last year.

5. The book _____ new information about John F. Kennedy's childhood.

Exercise 2 Complete the Sentences

These sentences have been started for you. They are not complete. Complete them with your own words.

1. Saving money is important. Moreover, _____

_____

_____

2. A driver's license will confirm a person's _____

_____

_____

3. A universal challenge for single parents is _____

_____

_____

4. Ronna's travel journal reveals _____

_____

_____

5. To use technology more effectively, I need to become more familiar with _____

_____

_____

Words at Work

Circle the best answer to each multiple choice question below. Then write a brief response to the question that follows. Write your answers in complete sentences.

---

1. Nina often travels to other cities for her job. Before she leaves home, she confirms her hotel reservation. Why does Nina do that?

   (A) to learn the address of the hotel

   (B) to make sure the hotel has her reservation

   (C) to change her reservation

   What are other details that can be confirmed when a person travels? _____

   _____

   _____

2. Erik asked everyone at work to give money to a charity that feeds poor families. What does this reveal about Erik?

   (A) He likes to cook for other people.

   (B) He cares about the lives of others.

   (C) He thinks his coworkers have too much money.

   Give another example of how people's actions reveal something about them. _____

   _____

   _____

3. Celine wrote a letter to the newspaper about the issue of graffiti. Here is part of her letter: "Graffiti is a universal problem in this city. It is in the park, on buildings, and on sidewalks. Moreover, it is on buses and traffic signs." Why does Celine think graffiti is a universal problem?

   (A) It is everywhere.

   (B) It damages city property.

   (C) It can be prevented.

   Think about your city. Is there a universal issue? What is it? _____

   _____

   _____

4. Cheryl's job is to confirm that information in accident reports is accurate. How does she do that?

   (A) She asks a coworker to read the reports.

   (B) She reads old accident reports.

   (C) She calls people listed in the accident report.

   When do you need to confirm important information at home, work, or school? _____

   _____

   _____

Word Families

Most words are part of a family of words. Study the word families on this page. Then fill in the missing words in the sentences below using the words from this lesson. Use the correct form of each word to complete the sentences.

---

confirm *(verb)*

- confirmation *(noun)*
  He received an e-mail confirmation of his class registration.

- confirmed *(adjective)*
  The hospital has three confirmed cases of the flu.

familiar *(adjective)*

- familiarity *(noun)*
  The governor's answers demonstrated his familiarity with the important issues.

- familiarize *(verb)*
  Ruben read the manual to familiarize himself with the new stamping machine.

reveal *(verb)*

- revealing *(adjective)*
  The magazine article provided revealing new details of the election.

- revelation *(noun)*
  The revelation that Angela was moving to Alaska surprised her friends.

universal *(adjective)*

- universally *(adverb)*
  Mother Teresa and Nelson Mandela are universally respected.

---

1. It was a _____ that our math teacher could sing so well.

2. The laboratory tests provided _____ that the dog had an infection.

3. The purpose of the brochure is to _____ people with the warning signs of a stroke.

4. Did the letter _____ that Brian's application was received?

5. Marriage is a _____ custom.

6. There was a _____ report of a tornado three miles away.

7. Jesse's _____ with snakes comes from working at the zoo for many years.

8. The text message provided _____ information to the police.

9. The Beatles are _____ popular.

10. Maya and Nelson _____ that they were expecting a new baby.

11. Are you _____ with the car's GPS?

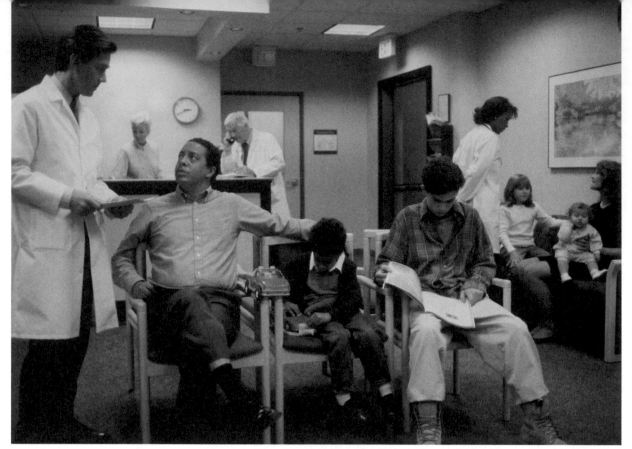

Health insurance makes it easier for everyone to get medical attention when they need it.

Exercise 5 What Do You Think?

Read each question and write a brief answer. Explain your answers in complete sentences.

---

1. Can universal healthcare prevent people from getting sick or having health issues?

_____

_____

_____

2. Is it necessary to be familiar with photography to take a good picture?

_____

_____

_____

3. Should a television reporter confirm the accuracy of a story before revealing it?

_____

_____

_____

Reading Connection

Read the following passage and answer the questions.

The Story of Icarus

The Story of Icarus *is a myth from ancient Greece. A myth is a story that is not true and has been told over and over for a long time. The purpose of a myth is to explain a universal idea or truth. As you read, try to find the universal idea that* The Story of Icarus *demonstrates.*

A long time ago, there was a powerful king named Minos. King Minos lived in a palace on the island of Crete. The king kept a terrible beast called a Minotaur in a separate part of the palace. A man named Daedalus built the part of the palace where the Minotaur lived. Daedalus was a great architect and inventor.

When Daedalus's work was done, he wanted to go home to Athens. However, King Minos would not let him. He kept Daedalus and his son Icarus as prisoners in a tower of the palace. The king made Daedalus invent weapons for him to use against his enemies. Icarus hated living in the tower. He could not run and play as other boys did.

One day, Daedalus watched some birds fly through the sky and past the tower where he and Icarus lived. "Birds can fly because they have wings," he thought. "If Icarus and I had wings, we could fly back to Athens."

Daedalus decided to make wings for him and his son. He made the wings from wood, bird feathers, and beeswax. When the wings were finished, father and son put them on. They climbed to the highest part of the tower and flew away.

Daedalus told Icarus to be careful when he was flying. If he got too close to the sun, the wax would melt and the feathers would fall off. Icarus laughed. He was having great fun flying. He flew higher and higher in the sky.

Daedalus called to him, "Come down, Icarus! Don't fly too close to the sun!" The boy did not listen to his father. The wax on his wings began to melt. One by one, the feathers fell off. Then Icarus fell from the sky into the sea below and was lost.

Today the place near Crete where Icarus drowned is called the Sea of Icarus.

1. Why did King Minos prevent Daedalus and Icarus from leaving Crete?

_____

_____

2. What does the myth reveal about Icarus? Why didn't he listen to his father?

_____

_____

3. Does this myth reinforce a universal idea? What do you think it is?

_____

_____

accurate damage convince **confirm** issue
destroy **familiar** reveal amount definite
fundamental expand maximum **moreover**
reveal minimum accurate issue obvious
issue reinforce **universal** provide prevent

New Word List

☐ confirm

☐ familiar

☐ moreover

☐ reveal

☐ universal

Review Word List

☐ _____

☐ _____

☐ _____

☐ _____

☐ _____

Exercise 7 Writing Connection

Write a brief response to each question. Use words from this lesson or previous lessons in your answer. Write your answers in complete sentences.

Being a parent is a universal experience. Describe a situation with children that is similar for parents anywhere in the world. Reinforce your answer with specific examples.

_____

_____

_____

_____

_____

Your neighbor's son borrowed one of your tools. He reveals to you that he lost it. Moreover, he doesn't have a job. What should you do?

_____

_____

_____

_____

Exercise 8 Reflection

Think about the words you have studied in this lesson.

1. Which words did you enjoy learning? _____

2. Select one word and imagine where you will use the word. Explain the situation.

_____

_____

3. Which words do you still need help with? _____

4. Return to the Knowledge Rating Chart at the beginning of this lesson. Complete column 3. How have your responses changed?

Activity 1 Create Sentences

Write five statements about the picture. Your statements can describe what you see or give an opinion. You can select a sentence starter from the chart to help you create interesting and different sentences. Use one or more of the vocabulary words you studied in this unit in each sentence. You may also use words from previous units. Underline each vocabulary word you use.

Make an observation:	Give an opinion:
There is/there are...	I think that...
I notice that...	In my opinion,...
It seems that...	It is important/It is essential...

Examples: I notice that the buildings have been either <u>damaged</u> or <u>destroyed</u>.
I think the government should <u>examine</u> new buildings and make sure they are <u>reinforced</u>.

_____

_____

_____

_____

_____

_____

_____

WORD BANK

ACCURATE
AMOUNT
CONFIRM
CONVINCE
DAMAGE
DEFINITE
DESTROY
EXPAND
FAMILIAR
FUNDAMENTAL
ISSUE
MAXIMUM
MINIMUM
MOREOVER
OBVIOUS
PREVENT
PROVIDE
REINFORCE
REVEAL
UNIVERSAL

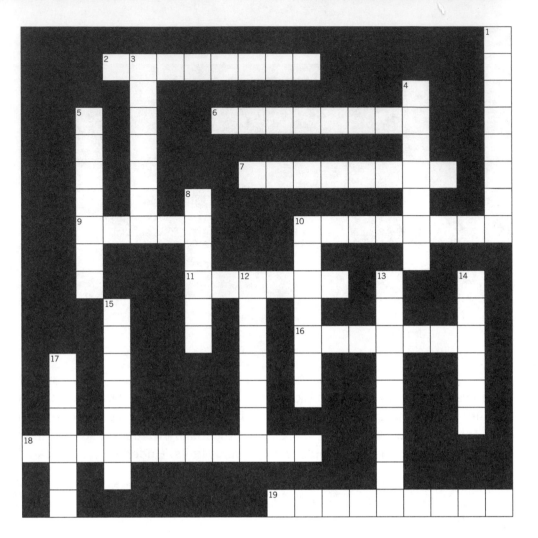

Activity 2 Puzzle

ACROSS

2. I can't _____ my father to change his mind.

6. If the information is _____, please sign your name.

7. You need to put a _____ time on the invitation.

9. The _____ of racism was the topic of Jackie's essay.

10. The pay is very good. _____, health insurance is provided.

11. I want to _____ the size of my vocabulary.

16. The visa permits you to stay for a _____ of 45 days.

18. There are _____ differences between boys and girls.

19. Music is a _____ language.

DOWN

1. The area is very _____ to me.

3. It was _____ that he missed his family.

4. How many acres did the forest fire _____?

5. I am calling to _____ my appointment.

8. Did the article _____ new information about the actor?

10. The vitamin label tells you the _____ daily requirement.

12. What can you do to _____ a cold?

13. It is important to _____ good behavior.

14. How much will it cost to repair the _____ to your car?

15. The company will _____ lunch today.

17. Can I decrease the _____ of sugar in this recipe?

Activity 3 Synonyms

Complete these sentences. Use the correct form of the vocabulary word that means the same as the word in parentheses.

Example: It is hot. _____Moreover_____, (*also*) we do not have enough water.

1. The fence _____ (*stopped*) the neighbor's dog from damaging our yard.

2. What is the _____ (*most*) number of pills I can take in one day?

3. The school _____ (*gave*) uniforms for all the players on the baseball team.

Activity 4 Antonyms

Complete these sentences. Use the correct form of the vocabulary word that means the opposite of the word in parentheses.

Example: We made _____definite_____ (*uncertain*) plans to visit Seattle this summer.

1. George's boss expects his reports to be _____ (*incorrect*) and neat.

2. When will the judges _____ (*hide*) the name of the winner in each category?

3. That girl looks _____ (*strange*), but I can't remember where I have seen her.

Activity 5 Practice Grammar with New Vocabulary

Rewrite the sentences. Change them from a declarative statement to a question.

Example: The owners want to expand their business outside of the state.
         Do the owners want to expand their business outside of the state*?*

1. The Secret Service provides protection for the president and his family. _____

_____

2. The doctor tried to convince her state representative of the need for universal healthcare.

_____

3. All of Priscilla's wedding photos were destroyed by the flood. _____

_____

4. Your hotel reservation has been confirmed. _____

_____

method minimum minor moreover neutral notice obvious option perform physical possess precise prevent previous process pro
ce refer reflect reinforce reject release require reveal reverse revise satisfy select severe significant similar site specific streng
gh topic transfer unique unite universal vision within accurate adequate adjust admit advantage among amount approval attitu
efit brief category challenge classify concern confidence confirm consider constant contain convince damage decrease define d
te deny depend essential evaluate examine expand expect familiar fit focus fundamental general glob
ase indicate maximum method minimum minor moreover neutral notice obvious option pe

Unit 4

unite
fit
among
site
disturb
individual
admit
reduce
define
unique
revise
minor
confidence
internal
contain
transfer
deny
indicate
concern
advantage.

advantage admit concern contain unite
among revise **define** confidence reduce
site **indicate** deny disturb internal admit
internal confidence unique define **minor** fit
contain unite **transfer** individual revise

Vocabulary Knowledge Rating Chart

How well do you know the words? Use the numbers to rate your knowledge of the vocabulary words. Follow the teacher's directions.

4 = I know the word. I know it well enough to teach it to someone else.
3 = The word is familiar. I think I know what it means.
2 = I have heard the word, but I'm not sure what it means.
1 = I don't know the word at all.

	My rating before instruction	I think the word means	My rating after instruction
advantage			
define			
indicate			
minor			
transfer			

Word Meaning Chart

Complete the chart. Follow the teacher's directions.

advantage *(noun)* /ad VAN tij/

An **advantage** helps or benefits you in some way.

EXAMPLES

Practicing before the game was a definite _____ for the team.

Class Example: _____

My Example: One of the **advantages** of having a car is _____

define *(verb)* /dih FAYHN/

To **define** is to describe something completely or to tell what something means.

EXAMPLES

The Constitution _____ the powers and responsibilities of Congress.

Class Example: _____

My Example: When a teacher clearly **defines** the class rules, _____

indicate *(verb)* /IN di keyt/

To **indicate** means to tell, show, or demonstrate.

EXAMPLES

Mr. King pointed up to _____ that the library was upstairs.

Class Example: _____

My Example: Smiling can **indicate** _____

minor *(adjective)* /MAHY ner/

Minor means small or not important.

EXAMPLES

The child did not need stitches because it was a _____ cut.

Class Example: _____

My Example: I made a **minor** mistake on my paper when _____

transfer *(verb)* /trans FUR/

To **transfer** means to move something or someone from one place to another.

EXAMPLES

When Mr. Birch is out, his assistant _____ his calls to Ms. Rosano's office.

Class Example: _____

My Example: I could not **transfer** the pictures to my computer, so _____

Exercise 1 Use the Words

Complete each sentence. Write the correct form of the vocabulary word in the blank space.

1. The sign _____ _____ that the clinic is open on Saturday mornings.

2. Ms. Watson _____ the old files from her office to the storage room last week.

3. Max was lucky. The accident only did _____ damage to his car.

4. Movies and television _____ American culture for many people around the world.

5. What is the _____ of living across the street from a fire station?

Exercise 2 Complete the Sentences

These sentences have been started for you. They are not complete. Complete them with your own words.

1. It is a challenge to transfer to a new school in the middle of the year because _____
_____
_____

2. I would define my city as _____
_____
_____

3. An example of a minor problem between neighbors is _____
_____
_____

4. One advantage of speaking more than one language is _____
_____
_____

5. When a person does not return a call, it could indicate _____
_____
_____

Words at Work

Circle the best answer to each multiple choice question below. Then write a brief response to the question that follows. Write your answers in complete sentences.

1. On her application, Marjorie wrote that she likes to swim, run, and play basketball. What do her activities indicate about her?

   (A) She watches sports on TV.   **(B)** She is an active person.   **(C)** She is not available to work weekends.

   Name some of your activities. What do your activities indicate about you? _____

   _____

   _____

2. Arthur defines himself as someone who is hardworking and loyal to his company. Which adjective would you use to define Arthur?

   (A) responsible   **(B)** active   **(C)** interested

   How would you define yourself as a student or worker? Explain or give an example. _____

   _____

   _____

   _____

3. One of Albert's tasks at work every morning is to transfer the pizza dough from the freezer to the refrigerator. He was late for work and forgot to do it today. Why is the cook upset?

   (A) The dough is too soft.   **(B)** The dough is too flat.   **(C)** The dough is too hard.

   What is something you transfer at home or at school? _____

   _____

   _____

4. Casey is a plumber. His body type is a definite advantage because he can easily crawl under houses to examine the pipes. What is Casey's advantage?

   (A) Casey is thin.   **(B)** Casey is tall.   **(C)** Casey has long legs.

   Give another example of a job in which body type can be important. _____

   _____

   _____

   _____

Word Families

Most words are part of a family of words. Study the word families on this page. Then fill in the missing words in the sentences below using the words from this lesson. Use the correct form of each word to complete the sentences.

---

advantage *(noun)*
• disadvantage *(noun, antonym)* Not being able to use a computer is a disadvantage when looking for a job.

define *(verb)*
• definition *(noun)* What is the definition of the word revelation?

indicate *(verb)*
• indication *(noun)* Dark clouds are often an indication of a storm.

transfer *(verb)*
• transfer *(noun)* Mr. Ming asked for a job transfer to a store that was closer to home.

1. Ricky forgot to get a bus _____, so he had to pay full fare.

2. The Depression and World War II _____ Franklin Roosevelt's presidency.

3. The increase in sales _____ that the company was performing better.

4. Lisa took _____ of living near her job by walking to work.

5. Shauna's perfect attendance _____ that she is very healthy.

6. Three of the team's players were sick, so the team was at a

   _____ when the tournament started.

7. Please read the _____ before answering the vocabulary question.

8. When is Marcia going to _____ the car registration to the new owner?

9. Alfredo's big smile was an _____ that he had passed the test.

10. Why did Felix ask for a _____ to a new school?

11. An apartment lease _____ the rights and responsibilities of the landlord and the tenant.

12. There are several _____ to having a library card.

Getting married is a major life event.

What Do You Think?

Read each question and write a brief answer. Explain your answers in complete sentences.

1. Is it an advantage for couples planning to get married to write a contract that defines their specific responsibilities?

_____

_____

_____

2. What does it indicate if a person is transferred often from one job to another? Could it indicate a problem?

_____

_____

_____

3. Is it an advantage to have a famous mother or father?

_____

_____

_____

The Executive Branch

The United States government is divided into three branches. They are the executive, the legislative, and the judicial branches. The executive branch includes the offices of the president, the vice president, and the cabinet. The president is the person in charge of the executive branch.

The president has a number of jobs and responsibilities. The president approves new laws that are passed by Congress. However, the president will not sign a law if he does not think it is effective.

The president is not able to manage all of his responsibilities alone. There are fifteen executive departments to help him. The head of each department is called a secretary, such as the secretary of defense or the secretary of transportation. The secretaries are members of the president's cabinet.

The president conducts the nation's business with other countries. He signs agreements with other nations. If there is a problem with another country, the president and the secretary of state work together to solve it.

Four million people work for the executive branch. That includes members of the armed forces. The president is the commander-in-chief of the armed forces.

Another important presidential job is to select Supreme Court justices, or judges. Congress has to approve the president's selections.

The Constitution lists three requirements to be president of the United States. The president must be at least 35 years old, a natural born citizen, and a U.S. resident for at least 14 years. That means that many people in the United States have the minimum requirements to be president.

1. What are two major responsibilities that define the role of the president in the government?

_____

_____

2. What is the advantage of having a cabinet?

_____

_____

3. What do the president's responsibilities indicate about the kind of experience a person needs for the job?

_____

_____

advantage admit concern contain unite
among revise **define** confidence reduce
site **indicate** deny disturb internal admit
internal confidence unique define **minor** fit
contain unite **transfer** individual revise

New Word List

☐ advantage

☐ define

☐ indicate

☐ minor

☐ transfer

Review Word List

☐ _____

☐ _____

☐ _____

☐ _____

☐ _____

Exercise 7 Writing Connection

Write a brief response to each question. Use words from this lesson or previous lessons in your answer. Write your answers in complete sentences.

Important events can define a generation or time in history. For some generations, it is a war, such as the Vietnam War. For others it is something spectacular like the moon landing. Reflect on the events of your generation. What event do you think will define your generation? Why?

_____

_____

_____

_____

_____

What are some indications that a supervisor is happy with a person's work?

_____

_____

_____

Exercise 8 Reflection

Think about the words you have studied in this lesson.

1. Which words did you enjoy learning? _____

2. Select one word and imagine where you will use the word. Explain the situation.

_____

_____

3. Which words do you still need help with? _____

4. Return to the Knowledge Rating Chart at the beginning of this lesson. Complete column 3. How have your responses changed?

advantage **admit** concern contain unite
among revise define confidence reduce
site indicate **deny** disturb internal admit
internal confidence unique define minor **fit**
contain unite transfer **individual** revise

Vocabulary Knowledge Rating Chart

How well do you know the words? Use the numbers to rate your knowledge of the vocabulary words. Follow the teacher's directions.

4 = I know the word. I know it well enough to teach it to someone else.
3 = The word is familiar. I think I know what it means.
2 = I have heard the word, but I'm not sure what it means.
1 = I don't know the word at all.

	My rating before instruction	I think the word means	My rating after instruction
admit			
among			
deny			
fit			
individual			

Word Meaning Chart

Complete the chart. Follow the teacher's directions.

---

admit *(verb)* /ad MIT/   To **admit** something is to agree that it is true.

EXAMPLES

The experienced actor _____ he still gets nervous before a performance.

Class Example: _____

My Example: I don't like to **admit** that _____

---

among *(preposition)* /uh MUHNG/   **Among** means in a group of people or things.

EXAMPLES

We camped _____ the tall pine trees so that we could enjoy the shade.

Class Example: _____

My Example: **Among** my friends, only I _____

---

deny *(verb)* /dih NAHY/   To **deny** something is to say that it is not true.

EXAMPLES

Ms. Ferguson _____ the rumor that she is leaving her job.

Class Example: _____

My Example: I was surprised when I heard my friend **deny** _____

---

fit *(verb)* /fit/   To **fit** means that a thing or a person matches another.

EXAMPLES

The punishment should _____ the crime.

Class Example: _____

My Example: _____ **fits** my idea of a fun birthday celebration.

---

individual *(adjective)* /in duh VIJ oo uhl/   **Individual** means one person or one item separate from a group.

EXAMPLES

Ice cream is only available in _____ servings at this store.

Class Example: _____

My Example: A teacher can meet the needs of **individual** students by _____

Exercise 1 — Use the Words

Complete each sentence. Write the correct form of the vocabulary word in the blank space.

1. Mother Teresa lived _____ the poor in India.

2. Would you like one large salad or six _____ salads?

3. Uncle Pat _____ he had a heart problem, so he did not take proper care of himself.

4. The jacket will keep me warm. Moreover, it _____ my budget.

5. Lucy _____ she lost the pearl bracelet and promised to replace it.

Exercise 2 — Complete the Sentences

These sentences have been started for you. They are not complete. Complete them with your own words.

1. I need individual help to _____

   _____

   _____

2. I admitted to my friends that I made a mistake when _____

   _____

   _____

3. Among U.S. presidents, Abraham Lincoln is one of the most famous because

   _____

   _____

   _____

4. A person who fits my definition of success has _____

   _____

   _____

5. The governor denied that _____

   _____

   _____

   _____

Words at Work

Circle the best answer to each multiple choice question below. Then write a brief response to the question that follows. Write your answers in complete sentences.

---

1. Lester asked his coworker Howard to work for him last Saturday. Howard agreed, but he did not show up. Moreover, Howard denied that he had promised to work for Lester. What did Lester learn about Howard?

   (A) Howard will keep a promise.

   (B) Howard is not responsible.

   (C) Howard is honest.

   When has someone denied something you knew was true? How did you feel? _____

   _____

   _____

2. Jake's skills and experience did not fit the description of the job he wanted. However, Jake chose to complete the application for the job. What was the result?

   (A) He didn't get hired.

   (B) He got an interview.

   (C) He had an advantage.

   Why is it important to make sure your skills fit the job? _____

   _____

   _____

3. Among all the supervisors, Charlene's favorite is Mr. Carter. One reason is because

   (A) Mr. Carter prevents employees from working overtime.

   (B) Mr. Carter expects employees to work overtime.

   (C) Mr. Carter gives employees the option to work overtime.

   Among your supervisors or teachers, who is your favorite? Give two reasons why. _____

   _____

   _____

4. The sales staff had a meeting. The manager wants the sales staff to give customers more individual attention. What can they do to better serve their customers?

   (A) say the same thing to every customer

   (B) ask customers about their specific needs

   (C) tell customers to come back later

   Describe the individual attention you would like from salespeople when you are shopping.

   _____

   _____

Word Families

Most words are part of a family of words. Study the word families on this page. Then fill in the missing words in the sentences below using the words from this lesson. Use the correct form of each word to complete the sentences.

---

admit *(verb)*
- **admission** *(noun)*
  The student's admission of cheating on the exam upset his parents.

deny *(verb)*
- **denial** *(noun)*
  John was in denial that he had caused the accident.

fit *(verb)*
- **fit** *(noun)*
  With your computer skills, this job is a good fit for you.
- **fit** *(adjective)*
  This house is fit for a queen!

individual *(adjective)*
- **individually** *(adverb)*
  Ms. Ling spoke individually to each applicant.

---

1. Nancy's emotional _____ did not convince the judge.

2. The scary movie was not _____ for children.

3. Blanche cleaned each piece of silver _____ before the party.

4. Anouk _____ that she forgot to pick up the clothes from the dry cleaner.

5. _____ rates for insurance are more expensive than group rates.

6. Is Thomas a good _____ with the rest of the players on the team?

7. Customers expected an _____ of responsibility from the compnay for the problem with the batteries.

8. The new computer _____ our needs perfectly.

9. Why did Peter _____ he forgot to buy the tickets for the concert?

10. Ms. Ortiz makes sure to meet with each student _____.

11. It is best to _____ your mistake and apologize.

12. The reporters questioned the mayor's _____ that he was involved in the scandal.

Birthdays are a time to celebrate among family and friends.

Exercise 5 What Do You Think?

Read each question and write a brief answer. Explain your answers in complete sentences.

1. Would you ever deny how old you are? Provide two reasons why people may refuse to admit their age.

_____

_____

_____

2. Is being a nurse a good fit for someone who prefers working with people individually or for someone who enjoys working among many different people?

_____

_____

_____

3. Is it easier to admit guilt when you are among friends or among strangers?

_____

_____

_____

Reading Connection

Read the following passage and answer the questions.

The Invention of Basketball

What sport can be played inside during the cold winter months? That was the challenge for James Naismith in 1891. Naismith was a physical education teacher at the YMCA Training School in Springfield, Massachusetts. The director asked him to create a new indoor game for young men to play in the school gymnasium. The new game had to be free of rough activity.

Naismith considered the popular outdoor sports of the time—football, baseball, and soccer. He also reflected on a game he played as a child in Canada. In this game, tossing a stone so that it went higher and slower was an advantage.

Naismith took ideas from those games to create a new sport. He called it Basket Ball. The first game was played with a soccer ball and two wooden baskets nailed to the gym walls. Naismith had 18 students in his class. He made two teams. Each team had nine players. Players tried to score by throwing the ball into one of the baskets.

Basketball was an immediate success. Many colleges started teams. Soon there were professional teams. The popularity of the game increased rapidly. It became a major college sport. In 1936, basketball became an Olympic sport. By the 1960s, most major cities in the United States had a professional basketball team. Some individual basketball players became very famous. Kareem Abdul-Jabbar, Michael Jordan, and Kobe Bryant are a few of the most famous basketball players.

Today basketball is played by men and women around the world. The sport James Naismith invented has changed over the years, but it is as popular as ever.

1. What are two similarities and differences between basketball today and Basket Ball in 1891?

   _____

   _____

2. Basketball players are among the most famous athletes in the country. What could be a reason for their popularity?

   _____

   _____

3. Basketball is a team sport. In what ways are individual players important to the success of the team?

   _____

   _____

advantage **admit** concern contain unite
among revise define confidence reduce
site indicate **deny** disturb internal admit
internal confidence unique define minor **fit**
contain unite transfer **individual** revise

New Word List

☐ admit

☐ among

☐ deny

☐ fit

☐ individual

Review Word List

☐ _____

☐ _____

☐ _____

☐ _____

☐ _____

Writing Connection

Write a brief response to each question. Use words from this lesson or previous lessons in your answer. Write your answers in complete sentences.

Which is a better fit for you, individual or team sports? Name a specific sport that fits you. Explain why it is a good fit for your personality and abilities.

_____

_____

_____

_____

_____

Your good friend Kyle admits that he has lost his job again. It is obvious that it is difficult for him to get to work on time. He denies that this problem is the reason for losing his job. What are some things he can do?

_____

_____

_____

_____

Exercise 8 # Reflection

Think about the words you have studied in this lesson.

1. Which words did you enjoy learning? _____

2. Select one word and imagine where you will use the word. Explain the situation.

_____

_____

3. Which words do you still need help with? _____

4. Return to the Knowledge Rating Chart at the beginning of this lesson. Complete column 3. How have your responses changed?

advantage admit contain **concern** unite
among **confidence** revise define reduce
site indicate deny **disturb** internal admit
internal confidence unique define minor fit
contain unite transfer individual deny **revise**

Vocabulary Knowledge Rating Chart

How well do you know the words? Use the numbers to rate your knowledge of the vocabulary words. Follow the teacher's directions.

4 = I know the word. I know it well enough to teach it to someone else.
3 = The word is familiar. I think I know what it means.
2 = I have heard the word, but I'm not sure what it means.
1 = I don't know the word at all.

	My rating before instruction	I think the word means	My rating after instruction
concern			
confidence			
disturb			
internal			
revise			

Word Meaning Chart

Complete the chart. Follow the teacher's directions.

---

concern *(noun)* /kuhn SURN/ — A **concern** is something that causes worry.

Preventing war is a universal _____.

Class Example: _____

My Example: A **concern** I have about my education is _____

---

confidence *(noun)* /KON fi duhns/ — **Confidence** is the belief that someone can do something well.

Uncle Charlie isn't worried about the operation because he has _____ in the doctor.

Class Example: _____

My Example: A teacher can demonstrate **confidence** in a student by _____

---

disturb *(verb)* /dih STURB/ — To **disturb** is to interrupt or upset someone or something.

Last night, barking dogs _____ our sleep.

Class Example: _____

My Example: When I study, one thing that **disturbs** me is _____

---

internal *(adjective)* /in TUR nl/ — **Internal** means that something is inside or occurs in something else.

Rudy's fall from the ladder caused _____ bleeding.

Class Example: _____

My Example: **Internal** communication in a school can be between _____

---

revise *(verb)* /ri VAHYZ/ — To **revise** something is to correct or change it.

Good writers _____ their work several times to make it better.

Class Example: _____

My Example: We had to **revise** our travel plans because _____

Exercise 1   Use the Words

Complete each sentence. Write the correct form of the vocabulary word in the blank space.

1. A warning label on some medicines says, "Not for _____ use."

2. Training gave Roy the _____ he needed to run in the marathon.

3. The state needs to _____ its budget and spend less next year.

4. Do the neighbors have _____ about the safety of the park?

5. "When you clean the patio, do not _____ the flower pots," said Mrs. Miller.

Exercise 2   Complete the Sentences

These sentences have been started for you. They are not complete. Complete them with your own words.

1. A major environmental concern is _____

_____

_____

2. A law that should be revised is _____

_____

_____

3. Writing in a diary is like having an internal conversation because _____

_____

_____

_____

4. A topic that disturbs me is _____

_____

_____

5. I do not have confidence in someone who _____

_____

_____

Words at Work

Circle the best answer to each multiple choice question below. Then write a brief response to the question that follows. Write your answers in complete sentences.

---

1. Della likes her coworkers. However, they sometimes disturb her while she is working. What should she tell them?

   (A) "Can't you see I'm working?"

   (B) "Be quiet! I'm busy."

   (C) "Sorry, I can't talk right now."

   What do you do when someone disturbs you while you're working or studying? _____

   _____

   _____

   _____

2. Mr. Park's crew measured the parking lot they were paving. He looked at his plan and told the crew to stop working. What was Mr. Park's concern?

   (A) The measurements were not accurate.

   (B) The parking lot was too big.

   (C) The measurements were accurate.

   When have you stopped working on a project because you had a concern? Why? _____

   _____

   _____

   _____

3. Samantha asked Indira to help her revise an accident report she must give to her supervisor. How can Indira help Samantha?

   (A) write the report

   (B) rewrite the report

   (C) suggest changes to improve the report

   What is something you have had to revise? Did someone help you? _____

   _____

   _____

4. Walter was glad to hire Ali to work in his store. Why does he have confidence in Ali?

   (A) Ali has experience.

   (B) Ali works weekends.

   (C) Ali is quite friendly.

   Who is someone you have confidence in? Explain why. _____

   _____

   _____

Word Families

Most words are part of a family of words. Study the word families on this page. Then fill in the missing words in the sentences below using the words from this lesson. Use the correct form of each word to complete the sentences.

---

concern *(noun)*

- concerned *(adjective)*
  The concerned parent asked to speak to the principal.

- concern *(verb)*
  It concerns me that the cost of insurance is so high.

confidence *(noun)*

- confident *(adjective)*
  Marilyn is confident that she will get her nursing license.

disturb *(verb)*

- disturbance *(noun)*
  Security questioned two people about a disturbance at the bank.

- disturbing *(adjective)*
  We read a disturbing article about global warming.

revise *(verb)*

- revision *(noun)*
  Leonard made several minor revisions to his speech.

- revised *(adjective)*
  The revised bus schedule is available online.

---

1. The newspaper showed some _____ pictures of animal cruelty.

2. Luis gave his client a _____ estimate for the cost of new appliances.

3. The _____ husband asked the nurse about his wife's condition.

4. Norman is _____ that he can lose weight with his new diet plan.

5. The _____ at the school dance was noisy but brief.

6. What did you think of the _____ to Marty's poem?

7. Tears indicated the child's obvious _____ for the kitten in the tree.

8. Many people don't have _____ in the nation's banking system.

9. Is recycling an issue that should _____ people?

10. The noise from the lawnmower _____ the sleeping baby.

11. Trisha needs to _____ her resume before she applies for any jobs.

Friends feel confident talking openly to each other.

Exercise 5 ## What Do You Think?

Read each question and write a brief answer. Explain your answers in complete sentences.

1. Is a friend someone you can always expect to share your concerns with? Reflect on your own experiences.

_____

_____

_____

2. Can a leader be effective without having the confidence of the people?

_____

_____

_____

3. Do you have more confidence in a person who rarely revises plans or a person who often revises plans?

_____

_____

_____

Reading Connection

Read the following passage and answer the questions.

What is a Cell?

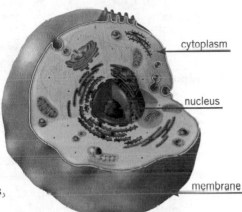

cytoplasm

nucleus

membrane

You can't see them, but your body is full of cells. In fact, you have about 100 trillion (100,000,000,000,000) of them! A cell is the smallest unit of living matter. A cell is so small that you need a microscope to see it.

A living thing is called an organism. People, animals, and plants are organisms. All organisms are made up of cells. Some organisms are only one cell. Bacteria and amoebas are examples of one-celled organisms. Humans and other organisms, however, are made up of millions or trillions of cells.

There are three major parts of a cell: the membrane, the cytoplasm, and the nucleus. The membrane is the outside wall of a cell. It protects the cell. The inside of a cell is filled with cytoplasm. Cytoplasm is a jelly-like substance made of water and nutrients. The nucleus is in the middle of the cell. The nucleus tells a cell what to do. The nucleus is often called the command center of a cell.

Each part of the human body is made up of different cells. The different cells have different jobs to do. Bone cells, for example, make bones that support the body. Blood cells fight disease and infection. Nerve cells let you feel pain or temperature. Other cells change food into the energy the body needs to live.

Cells die just as all living things do. White blood cells live for only 13 days. Liver cells live for about 18 months. Nerve cells, however, can live up to 100 years. Cells may be so tiny we can't see them, but we could not live without them.

1. What are the internal parts of a cell?

_____

_____

_____

2. Cells perform essential tasks in the human body. Name one type of cell and the task it performs.

_____

_____

_____

3. A doctor is concerned about a sick patient. Which cells will indicate to the doctor that the patient has an infection?

_____

_____

advantage admit contain **concern** unite
among **confidence** revise define reduce
site indicate deny **disturb** internal admit
internal confidence unique define minor fit
contain unite transfer individual deny **revise**

New Word List

☐ concern

☐ confidence

☐ disturb

☐ internal

☐ revise

Review Word List

☐ _____

☐ _____

☐ _____

☐ _____

☐ _____

Exercise 7 Writing Connection

Write a brief response to each question. Use words from this lesson or previous lessons in your answer. Write your answers in complete sentences.

Reflect on a time when you revised your opinion about an individual or an issue. Who or what was it? What changed your mind?

_____

_____

_____

_____

_____

Think about life in the 21st century. What do you think will concern people 50 years from now? Explain why.

_____

_____

_____

_____

_____

_____

Exercise 8 Reflection

Think about the words you have studied in this lesson.

1. Which words did you enjoy learning? _____

2. Select one word and imagine where you will use the word. Explain the situation.

_____

_____

3. Which words do you still need help with? _____

4. Return to the Knowledge Rating Chart at the beginning of this lesson. Complete column 3. How have your responses changed?

advantage admit **contain** concern unite
among revise define confidence **reduce**
site indicate deny disturb internal admit
internal confidence **unique** define minor fit
contain **unite** transfer individual revise

Vocabulary Knowledge Rating Chart

How well do you know the words? Use the numbers to rate your knowledge of the vocabulary words. Follow the teacher's directions.

4 = I know the word. I know it well enough to teach it to someone else.
3 = The word is familiar. I think I know what it means.
2 = I have heard the word, but I'm not sure what it means.
1 = I don't know the word at all.

	My rating before instruction	I think the word means	My rating after instruction
contain			
reduce			
site			
unique			
unite			

Word Meaning Chart

Complete the chart. Follow the teacher's directions.

contain *(verb)* /kuhn TEYN/
To **contain** means to have something inside.

EXAMPLES

Bananas _____ natural sugars and fiber.

Class Example: _____

My Example: My wallet or purse **contains** _____

reduce *(verb)* /ri DOOS/
To **reduce** means to make smaller in size or amount.

EXAMPLES

Stern's Office Supply _____ the price of many items this week.

Class Example: _____

My Example: I **reduce** the amount of electricity I use by _____

site *(noun)* /sahyt/
A **site** is a place where something is located or where something happened.

EXAMPLES

The paramedics quickly arrived at the _____ of the accident.

Class Example: _____

My Example: A historical **site** in our city is _____

unique *(adjective)* /yoo NEEK/
Unique means one of a kind or very special.

EXAMPLES

We are all different. Each of us is a _____ individual.

Class Example: _____

My Example: A **unique** way to celebrate a Valentine's Day is _____

unite *(verb)* /yoo NAHYT/
To **unite** means to join together for a common purpose.

EXAMPLES

After the flood, several organizations _____ to help with the clean up.

Class Example: _____

My Example: A way the Internet **unites** families and friends is _____

Exercise 1 Use the Words

Complete each sentence. Write the correct form of the vocabulary word in the blank space.

1. The doctor told Herb to _____ the amount of salt in his diet.

2. Helen loved to knit. She made _____ gifts for each of her friends.

3. My mother tried to _____ her tears of joy during my wedding.

4. In 1776, thirteen American colonies _____ to declare their independence.

5. Niagara Falls is a popular _____ for honeymoons.

Exercise 2 Complete the Sentences

These sentences have been started for you. They are not complete. Complete them with your own words.

1. I do not like movies that contain _____

2. An ideal site for a family reunion is _____

3. Music often unites people because _____

4. One way to reduce accidents at home is _____

5. My family is unique because _____

Words at Work

Circle the best answer to each multiple choice question below. Then write a brief response to the question that follows. Write your answers in complete sentences.

---

1. Nadia has to go to a union meeting. The site of the meeting is at a different location than where she works. What does she have to do?

   (A) go to the 10ᵗʰ floor   **(B)** take a bus   **(C)** go to the meeting room downstairs

   What is the advantage or disadvantage of working or taking classes at more than one site?

   _____

   _____

   _____

2. Jasmine applied to several colleges. Today she received a letter from one of the colleges. She was quite happy when she read the letter. What news did the letter contain?

   (A) She made a mistake on her application.   **(B)** She was not accepted.   **(C)** She got a scholarship.

   When have you received a letter that contained positive information? _____

   _____

   _____

3. Mrs. Patel asked her students to write a paragraph about a person who has a unique job. Who did Daniel write about?

   (A) a man who photographs farm animals   **(B)** a man who sells used cars   **(C)** a woman who works in a high-rise building

   Describe a unique job that someone you know has. _____

   _____

   _____

4. Anthony is a community organizer. Part of his job is to unite different neighborhood groups to focus on solving problems in the community. What is an essential skill for Anthony to possess?

   (A) listening carefully   **(B)** driving a car   **(C)** organizing files

   What is a reason for people in a neighborhood to unite? _____

   _____

   _____

Word Families

Most words are part of a family of words. Study the word families on this page. Then fill in the missing words in the sentences below using the words from this lesson. Use the correct form of each word to complete the sentences.

---

contain *(verb)*

- container *(noun)*
  We kept the salad in a plastic container in the refrigerator.

reduce *(verb)*

- reduction *(noun)*
  There was a 5 percent reduction in the city's air pollution last year.

unique *(adjective)*

- uniquely *(adverb)*
  Jazz is a uniquely American form of music.

unite *(verb)*

- united *(adjective)*
  The school is united in its goal to raise money for the tornado victims.

- unity *(noun)*
  The festival celebrates unity among different people of the world.

---

1. The library is closed on Tuesdays because of a new budget _____.

2. What _____ boots you are wearing! I have never seen a pair like that.

3. Should I _____ the oven temperature before I put the cake in?

4. The holiday decorations are stored in a large _____ in the garage.

5. The _____ workers voted to accept the new contract.

6. Sugar-free means that something does not _____ sugar.

7. The festival of Mardi Gras is _____ celebrated in New Orleans.

8. Family _____ helped everyone through the crisis.

9. The class was quite happy when the teacher _____ the amount of homework.

10. The candidate tried very hard to _____ his own political party.

11. Was Dr. Hart pleased with the _____ in David's cholesterol?

12. The human hand _____ 27 bones.

13. The coach told the newspaper that team _____ was the reason for its success.

Rovers on Mars search for water and collect scientific information.

What Do You Think?

Read each question and write a brief answer. Explain your answer in complete sentences.

1. Is it essential to know if there are sites on Mars that contain water?

_____

_____

_____

2. Is it a challenge for Americans to reduce the amount of foods they eat that contain sugar?

_____

_____

_____

3. Are unique events like natural disasters the only way for different groups of people to unite?

_____

_____

_____

Reading Connection

Read the following passage and answer the questions.

Island Paradise

Hawaii is the only state in the United States that is completely surrounded by water. Hawaii is a chain of islands in the Pacific Ocean. The chain stretches for more than 1,500 miles across the Pacific.

The Hawaiian Islands are actually the tops of huge volcanic mountains. There are eight major islands. They are Hawaii, Maui, Kahoolawe, Molokai, Lanai, Oahu, Kauai, and Niihau. People live on all the major islands except Kahoolawe. There are also 124 small islands that are part of the chain.

Hawaii is a unique state. It has two active volcanoes, Mauna Loa and Kilauea. They are located on the big island of Hawaii. The state of Hawaii also contains the wettest place on Earth. Mount Waialeale on the island of Kauai gets 460 inches of rain every year. It's no wonder Kauai is called the "Garden Island."

Tourism is the major industry of the Hawaiian Islands. People like Hawaii because of the mild tropical climate, gentle breezes, and natural beauty. The islands are famous for their surfing beaches. Agriculture is another important industry. Pineapples and sugarcane are grown in Hawaii. It is also famous as the birthplace of President Barack Obama. He was born in Honolulu on August 4, 1961.

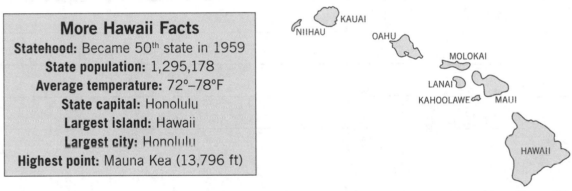

More Hawaii Facts
Statehood: Became 50th state in 1959
State population: 1,295,178
Average temperature: 72°–78°F
State capital: Honolulu
Largest island: Hawaii
Largest city: Honolulu
Highest point: Mauna Kea (13,796 ft)

1. Hawaii is the site of many unique things. Name two things that make Hawaii a unique state.

   _____

   _____

2. Did the passage about Hawaii contain new information for you? Did it confirm something you

   already knew? Tell what you learned or what was confirmed for you. _____

   _____

3. Are there advantages to living in a place like Hawaii? Are there disadvantages? What are they?

   _____

   _____

advantage admit **concern** contain unite
among revise define confidence **reduce**
site indicate deny disturb internal admit
internal confidence **unique** define minor fil
contain **unite** transfer individual revise

New Word List

☐ contain

☐ reduce

☐ site

☐ unique

☐ unite

Review Word List

☐ _____

☐ _____

☐ _____

☐ _____

☐ _____

Writing Connection

Write a brief response to each question. Use words from this lesson or previous lessons in your answer. Write your answers in complete sentences.

What does the slogan "United we stand, divided we fall" mean to you? Can you give an example?

_____

_____

_____

_____

_____

Think of someone you know who has a unique talent or ability. Describe it and tell why it is unique.

_____

_____

_____

_____

_____

_____

Reflection

Think about the words you have studied in this lesson.

1. Which words did you enjoy learning? _____

2. Select one word and imagine where you will use the word. Explain the situation.

_____

_____

3. Which words do you still need help with? _____

4. Return to the Knowledge Rating Chart at the beginning of this lesson. Complete column 3. How have your responses changed?

Activity 1 Create Sentences

Write five statements about the picture. Your statements can describe what you see or give an opinion. You can select a sentence starter from the chart to help you create interesting and different sentences. Use one or more of the vocabulary words you studied in this unit in each sentence. You may also use words from previous units. <u>Underline</u> each vocabulary word you use.

Make an observation:	Give an opinion:
There is/there are...	I think...
I notice that...	In my opinion...

Examples: The <u>site</u> of most basketball games is a gym or sports arena.
In my opinion, basketball is a <u>unique</u> sport.

_____

_____

_____

_____

_____

WORD BANK

ADMIT
ADVANTAGE
AMONG
CONCERN
CONFIDENCE
CONTAIN
DEFINE
DENY
DISTURB
FIT
INDICATE
INDIVIDUAL
INTERNAL
MINOR
REDUCE
REVISE
SITE
TRANSFER
UNIQUE
UNITE

Activity 2 Puzzle

ACROSS

1. It is a _____ surgery, so Bill is coming home after it.

3. Many people don't like to _____ their age.

6. Please call before 6:00, so you do not _____ our dinner.

9. I like your title. It is a good _____ for your story.

10. Bud could not _____ he was late. We all saw him.

12. Does the Constitution _____ the job of vice president?

14. _____ my son's teachers, only one is a man.

15. This cream is not for _____ use.

17. Does this pain pill _____ aspirin?

18. Get off at Grand Avenue and _____ to the Number 2 bus.

19. The unions need to _____ if they want political power.

20. Fewer cars on the road will _____ air pollution.

DOWN

2. Sue forgot to _____ the shift she wanted on the application.

4. The _____ rate for the policy costs more than the family rate.

5. The home team usually has an _____.

7. What a _____ dress! I've never seen one like it.

8. The increase in crime is a major _____.

11. This rock marks the _____ of a famous battle.

13. "I have _____ in you," the coach told the player.

16. Did you _____ the schedule for next week?

Activity 3 Synonyms

Complete these sentences. Use the correct form of the vocabulary word that means the same as the word in parentheses.

Example: Please do not _____disturb_____ (*bother*) Malcolm while he is studying.

1. The arrow _____ (*shows*) that the meeting is upstairs.

2. What is the _____ (*benefit*) of having two credit cards?

3. This box _____ (*holds*) all the cleaning supplies.

Activity 4 Antonyms

Complete these sentences. Use the correct form of the vocabulary word that means the opposite of the word in parentheses.

Example: The store _____decreased_____ (*increased*) its prices after the holiday.

1. The heart is an _____ (*external*) organ of the body.

2. It was a _____ (*major*) accident. There were only a few scratches.

3. The flower arrangement is beautiful and very _____ (*common*).

Activity 5 Practice Grammar with New Vocabulary

Rewrite the sentences. Change them from a declarative statement to a question using the question word in parentheses.

Example: Pauline admitted that she lost the keys. (*What*)
         What did Pauline admit? Or, What did Pauline admit having lost?

1. Art denied he damaged the mirror. (*What*) _____

   _____

2. Jeanne revised her essay at school this morning. (*Where*) _____

   _____

3. Mr. Rinaldi has a few concerns about the site for the new park. (*Who*) _____

   _____

4. The bank is going to transfer the money into Ramiro's account next week. (*When*) _____

   _____

Unit 5

precise
within
avoid
adjust
depend
general
significant
attitude
satisfy
strengthen
severe
method
neutral
constant
struggle
vision
classify
global
process
reverse

Lesson 17

classify adjust strengthen attitude reverse
avoid vision within **depend** method precise
reverse **general** constant neutral adjust
satisfy strengthen precise vision **process**
global severe **significant** within struggle

Vocabulary Knowledge Rating Chart

How well do you know the words? Use the numbers to rate your knowledge of the vocabulary words. Follow the teacher's directions.

4 = I know the word. I know it well enough to teach it to someone else.
3 = The word is familiar. I think I know what it means.
2 = I have heard the word, but I'm not sure what it means.
1 = I don't know the word at all.

	My rating before instruction	I think the word means	My rating after instruction
classify			
depend			
general			
process			
significant			

Word Meaning Chart

Complete the chart. Follow the teacher's directions.

classify *(verb)* /KLAS uh fahy/   To **classify** is to organize people or things into a group or category.

EXAMPLES

Scientists _____ living things as either animals or plants.

Class Example: _____

My Example: A library **classifies** _____

---

depend *(verb)* /dih PEND/   To **depend** on someone or something is to trust or need it to do something.

EXAMPLES

A child _____ on her parents for food and shelter.

Class Example: _____

My Example: To get to work, I **depend** on _____

---

general *(adjective)* /JEN er uhl/   The word **general** means not specific or detailed.

EXAMPLES

Ann has a _____ idea of where she wants to live but hasn't chosen a neighborhood.

Class Example: _____

My Example: I have **general** knowledge of _____, so I am not an expert.

---

process *(noun)* /PROS es/   A **process** is the way something is done or happens.

EXAMPLES

Selene got her picture taken as part of the _____ of getting her first passport.

Class Example: _____

My Example: One step in the registration **process** at school is _____

---

significant *(adjective)* /sig NIF i kuhnt/   The word **significant** means very important or having an important effect.

EXAMPLES

Heart disease is a _____ health problem in the United States.

Class Example: _____

My Example: Independence Day is a **significant** U.S. holiday because _____

Exercise 1   Use the Words

Complete each sentence. Write the correct form of the vocabulary word in the blank space.

1. Governors and mayors are selected through an election _____.

2. The government _____ certain information as secret.

3. The personal computer was a _____ invention of the 20th century.

4. The economy of Las Vegas _____ on tourism.

5. The topic *fish* is too _____ for a short essay. It needs to be more specific.

Exercise 2   Complete the Sentences

These sentences have been started for you. They are not complete. Complete them with your own words.

1. A significant experience in my life was _____

   _____

   _____

2. The general idea of soccer is to _____

   _____

   _____

3. One reason to classify people or things is _____

   _____

   _____

4. At home, I follow a process when I _____

   _____

   _____

   _____

5. People can depend on me to _____

   _____

   _____

   _____

Words at Work

Circle the best answer to each multiple choice question below. Then write a brief response to the question that follows. Write your answers in complete sentences.

1. Marylou has to create a process for selecting the employee of the month. What is an essential task for her to include?

   (A) define what "employee of the month" means

   (B) make a list of previous employees

   (C) hire new employees

   What is another step in the process? _____

   _____

   _____

2. Liz's daughter Sarah has homework. The homework is to classify a list of words. Sarah asks Liz to help her. How will they complete the homework?

   (A) write sentences with the words

   (B) make a puzzle with the words

   (C) put the words into categories

   What is something you classify at home, school, or work? _____

   _____

   _____

3. William wants to take a test to be an electrician. However, he only has a general knowledge of electricity from a previous job. Why is William worried about the test?

   (A) His previous job was in another state.

   (B) He has no specific knowledge of electricity.

   (C) He wants to study electricity.

   What is a job that requires specific knowledge? What is a job that requires general knowledge? Which type of job do you prefer?

   _____

   _____

4. Amira is applying for a scholarship. She must write an essay. The topic of the essay is "A Significant Challenge in My Life." What idea is she considering?

   (A) learning where the library is

   (B) learning how to speak English

   (C) learning how to use a dictionary

   What was a significant challenge in your life? _____

   _____

   _____

Exercise 4 — Word Families

Most words are part of a family of words. Study the word families on this page. Then fill in the missing words in the sentences below using the words from this lesson. Use the correct form of each word to complete the sentences.

---

classify *(verb)*

- classified ad *(noun)*
  Raul read the classified ads when he was looking for a job.

- classification *(noun)*
  The two basic classifications of wine are red and white.

depend *(verb)*

- dependent *(adjective)*
  Sylvia broke her leg and is dependent on her daughter to take her to the doctor.

- dependable *(adjective)*
  Sal's car is old, but it is dependable and gets him to work everyday.

general *(adjective)*

- generally *(adverb)*
  The weather in Southern California is generally sunny and warm.

process *(noun)*

- process *(verb)*
  It will take a week to 10 days to process your order.

significant *(adjective)*

- significantly *(adverb)*
  The new medicine significantly improved the child's health.

---

1. Do banks charge a fee to _____ a loan application?

2. Mothers _____ are protective of their children.

3. A _____ large number of people continue to smoke.

4. What job _____ best fits your skills?

5. David is a _____ person who always keeps his promises.

6. The FBI _____ armed robbery as a violent crime.

7. Lenore rides her bike to work some days. She doesn't like to be

   _____ on her car all the time.

8. The _____ of becoming a U.S. citizen takes time and requires patience.

9. The storm caused a _____ amount of damage.

10. Who can give me a _____ idea of where the library is?

11. Many retired people _____ on Social Security for all or part of their income.

Television is a "member" of the American family.

Exercise 5 ## What Do You Think?

Read each question and write a brief answer. Explain your answers in complete sentences.

1. American children generally watch about three hours of television a day. What significant results could that have?

_____

_____

_____

2. Have we become too dependent on computers to perform essential tasks?

_____

_____

_____

3. Is there ever a significant reason to classify people by race or religion?

_____

_____

_____

Suffixes

A suffix is a group of letters added to the end of a word. A suffix changes the part of speech.

The suffixes **-able** and **-ible** change a verb to an adjective.

adjust	adjustable
avoid	avoidable
depend	dependable
expand	expandable
prevent	preventable
notice	noticeable
reverse	reversible
transfer	transferable

The suffixes **-ance** and **-ence** change a verb or an adjective to a noun.

confident	confidence
depend	dependence
disturb	disturbance
perform	performance
refer	reference
significant	significance

The suffixes **-er**, **-or,** and **-r** change a verb to a noun.

contain	container
examine	examiner
indicate	indicator
perform	performer
provide	provider

The suffix **-ize** changes a noun or an adjective to a verb.

category	categorize
familiar	familiarize
general	generalize
internal	internalize
item	itemize
maximum	maximize
minimum	minimize
neutral	neutralize

The suffix **-ism** changes an adjective to a noun.

ideal	idealism

The suffixes **-ion**, **-sion,** and **-tion** change a verb to a noun.

admit	admission
classify	classification
confirm	confirmation
consider	consideration
define	definition
demonstrate	demonstration
destroy	destruction
examine	examination
evaluate	evaluation
expand	expansion
expect	expectation
indicate	indication
possess	possession
prevent	prevention
reduce	reduction
reflect	reflection
reject	rejection
reveal	revelation
revise	revision
satisfy	satisfaction
select	selection

The suffix **-ity** changes an adjective to a noun.

available	availability
familiar	familiarity
neutral	neutrality
severe	severity
similar	similarity

The suffix **-ment** changes a verb to a noun.

adjust	adjustment
reinforce	reinforcement
require	requirement

The suffix **-ness** changes an adjective to a noun.

unique	uniqueness
effective	effectiveness

Glossary/Index

Use the glossary to locate and review the vocabulary words you have learned in this book. As you move ahead in your vocabulary study, the glossary can be a useful reference.

accurate *(adj)*.................... Lesson 9
correct
- accuracy (n)   • accurately (adv)

adequate *(adj)*.................... Lesson 7
having enough of something, or something that is good enough
- adequately (adv)

adjust *(v)*.................... Lesson 18
to make small changes
- adjustment (n)   • adjustable (adj)

admit *(v)*.................... Lesson 14
to agree that something is true
- admission (n)

advantage *(n)*.................... Lesson 13
helps or benefits you in some way
- disadvantage (n)

among *(prep)*.................... Lesson 14
in a group of people or things

amount *(n)*.................... Lesson 9
a quantity of something

approval *(n)*.................... Lesson 7
agreement with an idea or action
- approve (v)

attitude *(n)*.................... Lesson 20
the opinions and feelings you have about a subject or a person

available *(adj)*.................... Lesson 8
free to do something or able to be used

avoid *(v)*.................... Lesson 18
to stay away or to prevent from happening
- avoidable (adj)   • unavoidable (adj)

benefit *(n)*.................... Lesson 5
something positive that improves life
- benefit (v)

brief *(adj)*.................... Lesson 1
short in length or time
- briefly (adv)

category *(n)*.................... Lesson 2
a group of people or things that are the same kind
- categorize (v)

challenge *(n)*.................... Lesson 5
something that is difficult
- challenging (adj)

classify *(v)*.................... Lesson 17
to organize people or things into a group or category
- classified ad (n)   • classification (n)

concern *(n)*.................... Lesson 15
something that causes worry
- concerned (adj)   • concern (v)

confidence *(n)*.................... Lesson 15
the belief that someone can do something well
- confident (adj)

confirm *(v)*.................... Lesson 12
to make sure that something is true or definite
- confirmation (n)   • confirmed (adj)

consider *(v)*.................... Lesson 7
to think very carefully before making a decision
- consideration (n)

constant *(adj)*.................... Lesson 18
regularly or all the time
- constantly (adv)

contain *(v)*.................... Lesson 16
to have something inside

convince (v)............... Lesson 11
to make someone believe that something is
true or necessary
- convinced (adj)   • convincing (adj)

damage (n)........................... Lesson 10
the harm that is done to something
- damage (v)

decrease (v)........................... Lesson 7
to become smaller in size, number,
or quantity
- decrease (n)

define (v)........................... Lesson 13
to describe something completely or to tell
what something means
- definition (n)

definite (adj)........................... Lesson 11
clear and certain
- definitely (adv)

demonstrate (v)........................... Lesson 6
to show something clearly
- demonstration (n)

deny (v)........................... Lesson 14
to say that something is not true
- denial (n)

depend (v)........................... Lesson 17
to trust or need someone or something
- dependent on (adj) • dependable (adj)

destroy (v)........................... Lesson 10
to damage something so it cannot be used or
does not exist
- destruction (n)   • destructive (adj)

disturb (v)........................... Lesson 15
to interrupt or upset someone or something
- disturbance (n)   • disturbing (adj)

effective (adj)........................... Lesson 3
getting a positive result
- effect (n)   • effectiveness (adj)
- effectively (adv)

essential (adj)........................... Lesson 4
important and necessary

evaluate (v)........................... Lesson 7
to judge how good or useful something is
- evaluation (n)

examine (v)........................... Lesson 3
to look at something carefully
- examination (n)   • exam (n)

expand (v)........................... Lesson 9
to become larger
- expansion (n)

expect (v)........................... Lesson 5
to have a good reason to think or believe
something will happen
- expectation (n)   • expected (adj)

familiar (adj)........................... Lesson 12
known from a previous time
- familiarity (n)   • familiarize (v)

fit (v)........................... Lesson 14
to match with another thing or person
- fit (n)   • fit (adj)

focus (v)........................... Lesson 8
to put close attention on one object, idea, or
person
- focus (n)   • focused (adj)

fundamental (adj)........................... Lesson 11
the most essential
- fundamentally (adv)

general (adj)........................... Lesson 17
not specific or detailed
- generally (adv)

global (adj)........................... Lesson 19
about or including the whole world
- globe (n)

however (adv)........................... Lesson 2
shows that what comes next is different from
what was said or done before

ideal *(adj)* .... Lesson 4
perfect or almost perfect

increase *(v)* .... Lesson 6
to become larger in number, size, or quantity
  • increase (n)

indicate *(v)* .... Lesson 13
to tell, show, or demonstrate
  • indication (n)

individual *(adj)* .... Lesson 14
separate from a group
  • individually (adv)

internal *(adj)* .... Lesson 15
inside or occurring inside something else

issue *(n)* .... Lesson 11
an important topic or problem

item *(n)* .... Lesson 1
one thing or object

major *(adj)* .... Lesson 6
very large, serious, or important

maximum *(adj)* .... Lesson 10
the greatest amount or size possible
  • maximum (n)

method *(n)* .... Lesson 19
a specific way of doing something
  • methodical (adj)

minimum *(adj)* .... Lesson 10
the smallest amount or size possible
  • minimum (n)

minor *(adj)* .... Lesson 13
small or not important

moreover *(adv)* .... Lesson 12
in addition

neutral *(adj)* .... Lesson 19
not choosing a side
  • neutrality (n)

notice *(v)* .... Lesson 3
to see, feel, smell, or hear something
or someone
  • notice (n)   • noticeable (adj)

obvious *(adj)* .... Lesson 9
easy to see or understand
  • obviously (adv)

option *(n)* .... Lesson 8
a choice
  • optional (adj)

perform *(v)* .... Lesson 4
to do an action or a job
  • performance (n)

physical *(adj)* .... Lesson 5
relates to the movement or feeling of the
body, or to something that can be seen
or touched
  • physically (adv)

possess *(v)* .... Lesson 8
to have or own something
  • possession (n)

precise *(adj)* .... Lesson 20
exact, definite, or clear
  • precisely (adv)

prevent *(v)* .... Lesson 10
to stop something from happening
  • prevention (n)

previous *(adj)* .... Lesson 1
one thing that happened before another
  • previously (adv)

process *(n)* .... Lesson 17
the way something is done or happens
  • process (v)

provide *(v)* .... Lesson 9
to give something or make it available
  • provider (n)

purpose *(n)* .... Lesson 3
the reason for something
  • on purpose (idiom)

quite (adv)............................ Lesson 8
very or a lot
- quite a few (idiom)   • quite a bit (idiom)
- not quite (idiom)

reduce (v)............................ Lesson 16
to make smaller in size or amount
- reduction (n)

refer (v)............................ Lesson 2
to get information from something
- reference (n)

reflect (v) .... Lesson 1
to think carefully about something
- reflection (n)

reinforce (v)............................ Lesson 11
to make something stronger
- reinforcement (n)

reject (v)............................ Lesson 6
to refuse to accept something
- rejection (n)

release (v)............................ Lesson 5
to free or let go of something or someone
- release (n)

require (v)............................ Lesson 4
to make something necessary
- requirement (n)   • required (n)

reveal (v) .... Lesson 12
to show what was not seen or known before
- revealing (adj)   • revelation (n)

reverse (v)............................ Lesson 20
to change something back to the way it was
- reversible (adj)

revise (v)............................ Lesson 15
to correct or change something
- revision (n)   • revised (adj)

satisfy (v)............................ Lesson 20
to meet the needs of someone or something
- satisfied (adj)   • satisfaction (n)
- satisfactory (adj)

select (v)............................ Lesson 2
to choose
- selection (n)

severe (adj)............................ Lesson 20
very bad or serious
- severely (adv)

significant (adj)............................ Lesson 17
very important or having an important effect
- significantly (adv)

similar (adv)............................ Lesson 3
almost the same, but not exactly
- similarity (n)

site (n)............................ Lesson 16
a place where something is located or where
something happened

specific (adj) .... Lesson 1
exact or clear
- specifically (adv)

strengthen (v)............................ Lesson 19
to make stronger or better
- strength (n)

struggle (v)............................ Lesson 19
to work hard to do something
- struggle (n)

task (n)............................ Lesson 4
a specific activity or job that needs to be done

through (prep)............................ Lesson 6
going from one end to another end
- through (adj)

topic (n)............................ Lesson 2
a big idea or subject

transfer (v)............................ Lesson 13
to move something or someone from one
place to another
- transfer (n)

unique (adj)............................ Lesson 16
one of a kind or very special

unite *(v)*.. Lesson 16
to join together for a common purpose

universal *(adj)*.................................... Lesson 12
common to everyone or available everywhere
  • universally (adv)

vision *(n)*.. Lesson 18
a mental picture of what something could be
  • envision (v)

within *(prep)*...................................... Lesson 18
during a time period or inside a place
or organization

Image Credits

V (inset)The McGraw-Hill Companies, Inc./Jacques Cornell photographer, (t)Getty Images/Blend Images; **3** Asia Images Group/Getty Images; **6** ASSOCIATED PRESS; **11** Momentum Creative Group/Alamy; **14** Lilly Dong/Getty Images; **19** Getty Images/Blend Images; **22** Peter Gridley / Getty Images; **27** S. Wanke/PhotoLink/Getty Images; **30** Stockbroker/SuperStock; **33** The McGraw-Hill Companies; **39** Allison Michael Orenstein/Getty Images; **42** JUPITERIMAGES/ Creatas/Alamy; **43** Corbis Premium RF/Alamy; **47** Comstock Images/Alamy; **51** The McGraw-Hill Companies; **53** Brand X Pictures/PunchStock; **55** Jupiterimages/Brand X Pictures/Getty Images; **58** Roll Call/Getty Images; **63** Getty Images, Inc.; **66** Michael Newman/PhotoEdit; **69** GREG RYAN/Alamy; **75** Tony Anderson/Getty Images; **78** U.S. Air Force photo by Master Sgt. Michael Farris; **83** Ilene MacDonald/Alamy; **86** Andersen Ross/Getty Images; **91** Guy Cali/CORBIS; **94** (l)Digital Vision/Getty Images, (c)ColorBlind Images/Getty Images, (r)Simon Battensby/Getty Images; **99** Royalty-Free/CORBIS; **102** Michael Malyszko/Getty Images; **105** Olivier Laban mattei/AFP/Getty Images; **111** Photodisc/PunchStock; **114** Brand X Pictures/PunchStock; **119** Royalty-Free/CORBIS; **122** Photodisc/Getty Images; **127** Ingram Publishing/SuperStock; **130** Flying Colours Ltd/Getty Images; **131** The McGraw-Hill Companies; **135** D. Falconer/PhotoLink/ Getty Images; **138** Stocktrek Images, Inc./Alamy; **139** The McGraw-Hill Companies; **141** U.S. Air Force; **147** Bananastock/Alamy; **150** Daniel Pangbourne/Digital Vision/Getty Images; **155** PhotoAlto/PunchStock; **158** Ariel Skelley/Getty Images; **163** Getty Images; **166** Royalty-Free/ CORBIS; **171** C Squared Studios/Getty Images; **174** (l)Jupiterimages/Getty Images, (r)Brand X Pictures; **177** Digital Vision/Getty Images.